Key Stage 3 Science Lab Book
Preparation for Pearson Edexcel GCSE (9-1)

Mark Levesley

Contents

Core skills grid	3
Biology	
Biology 1: Using microscopes	5
Biology 2: Investigating variation	12
Biology 3: Investigating photosynthesis	18
Biology 4: Yeast respiration	22
Chemistry	
Chemistry 1: Testing indigestion remedies	27
Chemistry 2: Separating mixtures	32
Chemistry 3: Investigating chemical reactions	39
Chemistry 4: Energy reactions	46
Physics	
Physics 1: Voltage, current and resistance	54
Physics 2: Investigating insulation	60
Physics 3: Investigating speed	66
Physics 4: Investigating electromagnets	72
Skills appendix	77

Published by Pearson Education Limited, 80 Strand, London, WC2R 0RL.

www.pearsonschoolsandfecolleges.co.uk

Copies of official specifications for all Pearson Edexcel qualifications may be found on the website: qualifications.pearson.com

Text © Mark Levesley, Ian Braid, Steve Gray, Sue Kearsey, Julian Clarke, Sue Robillard, Penny Johnson, Janet Murray, Sandra Baggley and Pearson Education Ltd.

Designed by Pete Stratton, Pearson Education Ltd
Typeset by Servis Filmsetting Ltd

Original illustrations © Pearson Education Ltd 2018

Cover design by Pete Stratton
Cover photo/illustration © Shutterstock: a_v_d

The rights of Mark Levesley, Ian Braid, Steve Gray, Sue Kearsey, Julian Clarke, Sue Robillard, Penny Johnson, Janet Murray, Sandra Baggley to be identified as authors of this work have been asserted by them in accordance with the Copyright, Designs and Patents Act 1988.

First published 2018

19 18
10 9 8 7 6 5 4 3 2 1

British Library Cataloguing in Publication Data

A catalogue record for this book is available from the British Library
ISBN 9781292256726

Copyright notice

All rights reserved. No part of this publication may be reproduced in any form or by any means (including photocopying or storing it in any medium by electronic means and whether or not transiently or incidentally to some other use of this publication) without the written permission of the copyright owner, except in accordance with the provisions of the Copyright, Designs and Patents Act 1988 or under the terms of a licence issued by the Copyright Licensing Agency, Barnards Inn, 86 Fetter Lane, London EC4A 1EN (www.cla.co.uk). Applications for the copyright owner's written permission should be addressed to the publisher.

All other media © Pearson Education Ltd

Printed in Italy by Lego S.p.A

Notes from the publisher

We have attempted to identify all the recognised hazards in the practical activities in this guide. The Lab Book and online Teacher and Technician Notes provide suitable warnings about the hazards and suggests appropriate precautions. Teachers and technicians should remember, however, that where there is a hazard, the employer is required to carry out a risk assessment under either the COSHH Regulations or the Management of Health and Safety at Work Regulations. We have assumed that practical work is carried out in a properly equipped and maintained laboratory and that any fieldwork takes account of the employer's guidelines. In particular, we have assumed that any mains-operated electrical equipment is properly maintained, that students have been shown how to conduct normal laboratory operations (such as heating or handling heavy objects) safely and that good practice is observed when chemicals or living organisms are handled. We have also assumed that classes are sufficiently small and well-behaved for a teacher to be able to exercise adequate supervision of the students and that rooms are not so crowded that students' activities pose a danger to their neighbours.

Science safety experts have reviewed but not trialled this text. Following receipt of the reviews any guidance has been incorporated and the resources updated.

Content accuracy

Pearson has robust editorial processes, including answer and fact checks, to ensure the accuracy of the content in this publication, and every effort is made to ensure this publication is free of errors. We are, however, only human, and occasionally errors do occur. Pearson is not liable for any misunderstandings that arise as a result of errors in this publication, but it is our priority to ensure that the content is accurate. If you spot an error, please do contact us at resourcescorrections@pearson.com so we can make sure it is corrected.

Introduction

KS3 Science Lab Book

This Lab Book has been designed to help you enjoy and feel confident about practical work in your science lessons. It covers 12 key practicals: four for biology, four for chemistry and four for physics. For each practical there are three sections:

- **Getting started** – an introduction to the practical with starter questions
- **Practical work** – apparatus, method and safety guidance for the practical, together with support around recording your results and drawing conclusions
- **Check your understanding** – questions to help you check your understanding and reflect on what you can do to further develop your skills.

There are spaces for you to write in your answers, results and conclusions, making this Lab Book a place for you to keep a full record of your work on these practicals. You will find it useful to refer back to this Lab Book in future for revision.

For each practical, key terms are placed in **bold**. You can find definitions for these by visiting **www.pearsonschools.co.uk/KS3LabGlossary**

The core skills grid on pages 3 and 4 can be used to help you track the practical skills you are developing as you work through this Lab Book. These are skills you will continue to use and build on throughout secondary science as you work towards GCSE. The Skills appendix at the back of this Lab Book will support you with these skills.

We hope that the experiments in this Lab Book encourage you to be curious about the world around you and to explore how scientists think and to discover what they do.

Note for teachers and technicians:

Comprehensive free online teacher and technician support is available at **www.pearsonschools.co.uk/KS3LabTeacherGuide** to help with the delivery of each practical, including a full set of answers and links to Exploring Science Working Scientifically, the KS3 National Curriculum, awarding organisation learning pathways and GCSE (9–1) specifications. Mapping grids are included to show how the core practical skills for this book have been derived from the GCSE (9–1) specifications.

Core skills grid

KS3 Science Lab Book

This grid lists 25 core skills you will develop as you work through your lab book. Developing these skills will help your scientific understanding and lay strong foundations for practical work at GCSE.

Core skill	Biology				Chemistry				Physics			
	1	2	3	4	1	2	3	4	1	2	3	4
Using scientific knowledge to test and develop ideas												
1 Plan experiments to make observations, and to test ideas and models.			✓	✓	✓	✓	✓	✓	✓		✓	✓
2 Describe how scientific hypotheses and theories develop and how scientists use peer-reviewed journals to publish their ideas.		✓	✓				✓			[✓]		✓
Planning experimental methods												
3 Identify hazards and plan ways to control risks during and/or after practical work.			✓		✓	✓	[✓]	[✓]				✓
4 Apply sampling techniques.		✓								✓	✓	
5 Identify and choose appropriate independent and dependent variables.				✓	✓	[✓]			✓	✓	✓	✓
6 Identify and plan to control appropriate control variables.				✓	✓	[✓]			✓	✓	✓	✓
Using apparatus												
7 Examine specimens using a microscope correctly.	✓											
8 Set up and use a Bunsen burner safely.				[✓]		✓		✓				
9 Separate mixtures of substances using appropriate techniques.						✓	✓	✓	✓		✓	[✓]
10 Use appropriate apparatus consistently to measure and record and explain differences between related measurements.		✓		✓	✓	[✓]	✓	✓	✓		✓	✓
Collecting and recording results												
11 Make sufficient observations and readings from measuring equipment, with consideration of an appropriate degree of detail, accuracy and precision.		✓			[✓]		[✓]	✓	✓		✓	[✓]

3

Core skills grid — KS3 Science Lab Book

Practicals

Core skill	Biology 1	Biology 2	Biology 3	Biology 4	Chemistry 1	Chemistry 2	Chemistry 3	Chemistry 4	Physics 1	Physics 2	Physics 3	Physics 4
12 Produce labelled drawings and diagrams.	✓					✓		✓	✓	✓		
13 Use and develop systematic tables in which to record observations and data.	✓				[✓]		[✓]	✓	[✓]	✓	[✓]	✓

Considering results and drawing conclusions

14 Use observations/collected data and scientific knowledge to draw conclusions.	[✓]	[✓]	✓	✓	[✓]	[✓]	✓	✓	✓	✓	✓	✓
15 Construct reasoned explanations for conclusions.		✓	✓	✓	[✓]	[✓]	✓	✓		✓		
16 Interpret and plot bar charts, line graphs and scatter graphs.		✓		✓						✓		
17 Use and rearrange equations/formulae to perform calculations.							✓		✓		✓	
18 Calculate means.		✓										
19 Present data to a certain degree of accuracy.							✓		✓		✓	
20 Identify patterns, correlations and linear relationships.		✓		✓				✓		✓	[✓]	[✓]
21 Identify anomalous results.		✓						✓			✓	
22 Use lines on graphs to estimate other values.			✓					✓		✓		
23 Use results and findings to develop further questions or ideas that can be tested.												

Evaluating experimental methods and results

24 Suggest ways to improve an experiment.	[✓]			✓				✓		✓	✓	
25 Suggest reasons for differences in repeat readings and suggest better ways to control variables.							✓			✓	✓	

✓ = a focus for this practical
[✓] = some coverage

Biology 1: Using microscopes

KS3 Science Lab Book

Getting started

Aims
- Use a light microscope to examine plant and animal tissues, and decide which is which.
- Prepare a microscope slide.

Skills you will develop
- ☐ Examine specimens using a microscope.
- ☐ Prepare slides.
- ☐ Use equations to perform calculations (for **magnification**).
- ☐ Produce labelled drawings and diagrams.

What you need to know before starting

✔ Identify the parts of animal and plant cells.

Robert Hooke was the first person to study tissues with a light microscope. In 1665, he examined the bark of a cork oak tree and saw little box shapes. He thought that they looked like the cells (small rooms) in a monastery and so that's what he called them.

Hooke's microscope had a magnification of about ×30. Modern light microscopes magnify up to about ×1500, but electron microscopes magnify up to about ×2 000 000.

Starter questions

1a Label the plant cell below with the names of its parts. Use words from the box.

cell membrane	cell wall	chloroplast
cytoplasm	nucleus	vacuole

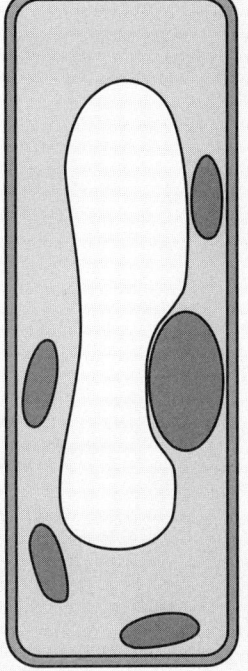

Top Tips
- Draw label lines with a ruler.
- Label lines should touch the part you are labelling.

b List the parts you would *not* find in an animal cell.

Glossary: www.pearsonschools.co.uk/KS3LabGlossary

Biology 1: Using microscopes

KS3 Science Lab Book

Practical work

Follow these instructions to obtain clear images of **specimens** using a light microscope. Then practise making your own specimen **slides**.

Experiment 1 Observing cells

Apparatus	Safety
• light microscope • two prepared slides • lamp (optional)	• Adjust microscope magnification with great care. • Do not angle mirrors towards the Sun, as this can seriously damage eyesight. • Be careful when handling microscope slides.

Method

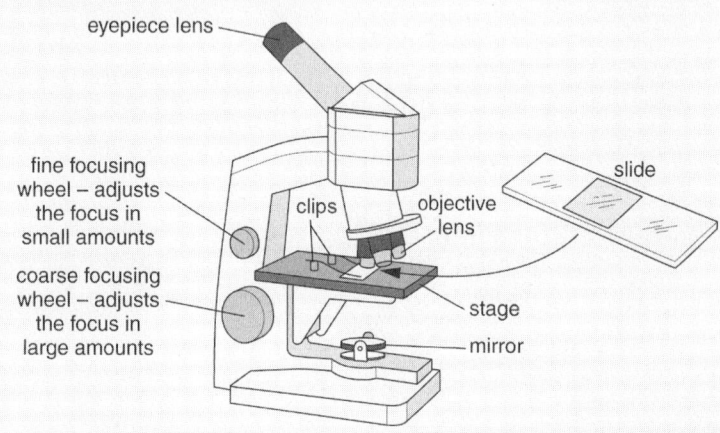

A Turn the **objective lenses** so that the lowest power lens is over the hole in the **stage**.

B Turn the large **coarse focusing wheel** to make the gap between the stage and the **objective lens** as small as possible.

C Place a slide on the stage. Use the clips to hold the slide in place.

D Adjust the **light source**. Either turn on the lamp or turn your mirror so that light is reflected up into the hole in the stage.

E Look into the **eyepiece lens**. It is best to look down a microscope with both eyes open. If you do this, your eyes will not get tired and you will see more.

F Turn the coarse focusing wheel slowly so that the gap between the stage and the objective lens gets bigger. Keep turning until what you see is clear (**in focus**).

G To see a bigger image, place the next most powerful objective lens over the specimen. Now, use only the **fine focusing wheel** to adjust the focus.

H Record the magnifications of the objective lens and eyepiece lens in the results section.

I Make a labelled drawing of what you see, in the results section. Record the name that is on the slide.

J Repeat steps **A** to **I** using a different slide.

> **Safety**
> Never point the mirror directly at the Sun. This can permanently damage your eyesight.

> **Safety**
> Do not use the coarse focusing wheel with higher power objectives. If you can't see anything, go back to a lower power objective and focus the slide again before returning to the higher power objective.

Glossary: www.pearsonschools.co.uk/KS3LabGlossary

Biology 1: Using microscopes

KS3 Science Lab Book

Recording your results

1a In the boxes, draw one or two of the cells that you observed.
  b Label the parts of the cells on your drawings.
  c Record the **magnifications** of the lenses that you used.

Slide 1
Name on slide: _____

Eyepiece lens magnification: _____

Objective lens magnification: _____

Slide 2
Name on slide: _____

Eyepiece lens magnification: _____

Objective lens magnification: _____

Glossary: www.pearsonschools.co.uk/KS3LabGlossary

Biology 1: Using microscopes

KS3 Science Lab Book

Considering your results / Conclusions

2a Are the cells in slide 1 from a plant or an animal? _____

b Describe how **evidence** from your results supports this conclusion. _____

_____

_____

c Calculate the total magnification used to observe slide 1. Use the **equation** below and show your working.

total magnification = eyepiece lens magnification × objective lens magnification

Calculating the total magnification for slide 1:

total magnification = _____ × _____

total magnification = _____

3a Are the cells in slide 2 from a plant or an animal? _____

> **Top Tip**
>
> For example, using a × 5 eyepiece and × 10 objective, the total magnification is 5 × 10 = 50.
>
> The image seen through the microscope is 50 times bigger than the real size of the specimen on the slide.

b Describe how evidence from your results supports this conclusion. _____

_____

_____

c Calculate the total magnification used to observe slide 2. Show your working.

total magnification = _____

Biology 1: Using microscopes

KS3 Science Lab Book

Experiment 2 Preparing slides

Apparatus	Safety
• light microscope • lamp • coverslip • stain (e.g. methylene blue) • pipette • slide • microscope • cotton bud • paper towels	• Adjust microscope magnification with great care. • Do not angle mirrors towards the Sun, as this can seriously damage eyesight. • Be careful when handling microscope slides. • Be careful with stains – they stain skin and clothes. • Place all used cotton buds, slides, etc., where your teacher shows you.

Prediction

A **prediction** is what you think you will find.

1 Read the method below. Then draw a picture of what you think you will find.

Method

A Put a drop of stain on a slide. A stain helps you to see certain parts of cells. 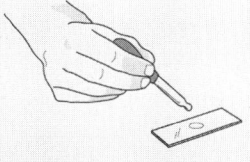	**B** Place a cotton bud against the inside of your cheek. Then take it out of your mouth. 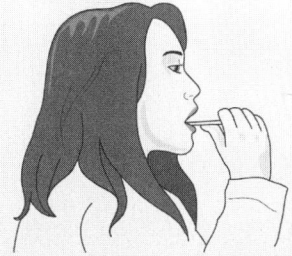

Glossary: www.pearsonschools.co.uk/KS3LabGlossary

Biology 1: Using microscopes

KS3 Science Lab Book

| C Dip the end of the cotton bud into the stain and stir gently. 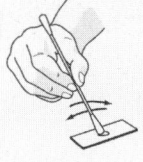 | D Place one side of a coverslip on the edge of the pool of stain, supporting the other side with the cotton bud. Slowly lower it (to avoid trapping air bubbles). The coverslip will stop the specimen drying out and will hold it in place. 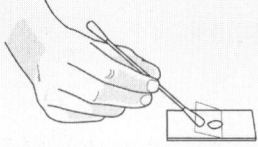 |

E Observe your cells under a microscope.

Recording your results

2 Draw what you see on your slide under the microscope. Add labels.

3 Write down the magnifications of the lenses you used to make your drawing.

eyepiece lens _____   objective lens _____

Considering your results / Conclusions

4 Calculate the total magnification you used. Show your working.

total magnification = _____

5a What did you see on your slide when using the microscope? _____

b Was this what you expected to see? _____

c If not, how was it different? _____

Glossary: www.pearsonschools.co.uk/KS3LabGlossary

Biology 1: Using microscopes

KS3 Science Lab Book

Check your understanding

1. Why do we use coverslips? Tick *two* reasons.
   - ☐ to squash a thick specimen
   - ☐ to hold a specimen in place
   - ☐ to add stain to a specimen
   - ☐ to stop a specimen drying out
   - ☐ to magnify a specimen
   - ☐ to let light through a specimen

2. Complete the missing magnifications in the table.

Magnification of eyepiece lens	Magnification of objective lens	Total magnification
×5	×10	
×5	×40	
×10		×150

3. Why do we use a stain?

   _____
   _____

4. A student just sees darkness when looking through their microscope. Describe what they could do in order to see the specimen.

   _____
   _____
   _____
   _____

Checkpoint

Teacher comments

Look at the 'Skills you will develop' on page 5. In the boxes, indicate how confident you are at each skill.

What I will do to develop my skills more

Glossary: www.pearsonschools.co.uk/KS3LabGlossary

Biology 2: Investigating variation

KS3 Science Lab Book

Getting started

Aim
- Look for a relationship between the height of a person and the volume of air in a normal breath.

Skills you will develop
- ☐ Describe how scientific hypotheses develop.
- ☐ Make sufficient, accurate observations.
- ☐ Draw reasoned conclusions from data.
- ☐ Calculate means.
- ☐ Interpret and plot charts/graphs (scatter graphs, including lines of best fit).
- ☐ Identify correlations/relationships.

What you need to know before starting
- ✔ Recall the main parts of the human breathing system.
- ✔ Recall some common units used to measure volumes and lengths.
- ✔ Recall the meanings of the terms: variable, variation.

A **hypothesis** is a scientific idea. It can be tested by doing experiments. It is *not* a question and nor does it have to be correct. It is just an idea about how or why something happens. For example:

a) Does water get hotter the longer you heat it?

b) The temperature of water depends on the length of time you heat it for.

> **Top Tips**
> - a) is a question.
> - b) is a hypothesis. Hypotheses can often be written using 'depends on' to link two **variables**.

Starter questions

1. Which of these is a hypothesis? Tick *one or more*.
   - ☐ The number of fish in a pond depends on the amount of oxygen in the water.
   - ☐ Does brushing your teeth make you less likely to need fillings?
   - ☐ Fewer seeds germinated when we gave them more acidic water.
   - ☐ The length of your legs depends on your height.
   - ☐ Athletes' heartbeat rates depend on how fast they are running.
   - ☐ Inhaled ('breathed in') air contains about 21% oxygen.

2. We use hypotheses to plan experiments and to make **predictions**. A prediction says what we think will happen in an experiment if a hypothesis is correct. For example:

   a) The temperature of water depends on the length of time you heat it for.

   b) If we heat the water for longer, it will have a higher temperature.

   An experiment tests the hypothesis that breathing rate depends on the intensity of exercise. Write a prediction to say what you think will be found.

> **Top Tips**
> - a) is a hypothesis.
> - b) is a prediction. Predictions can often be written using 'if ... then ...'

Glossary: www.pearsonschools.co.uk/KS3LabGlossary

Biology 2: Investigating variation

KS3 Science Lab Book

3 An investigation tested the hypothesis that people's arm lengths depend on their heights. The **scatter graph** shows a **correlation**: when one variable changes, so does the other. One measurement does not fit the pattern – it is **anomalous**.

> **Top Tip**
> Find help on scatter graphs, lines of best fit, correlations and anomalous **data** in the Appendix (section S18).

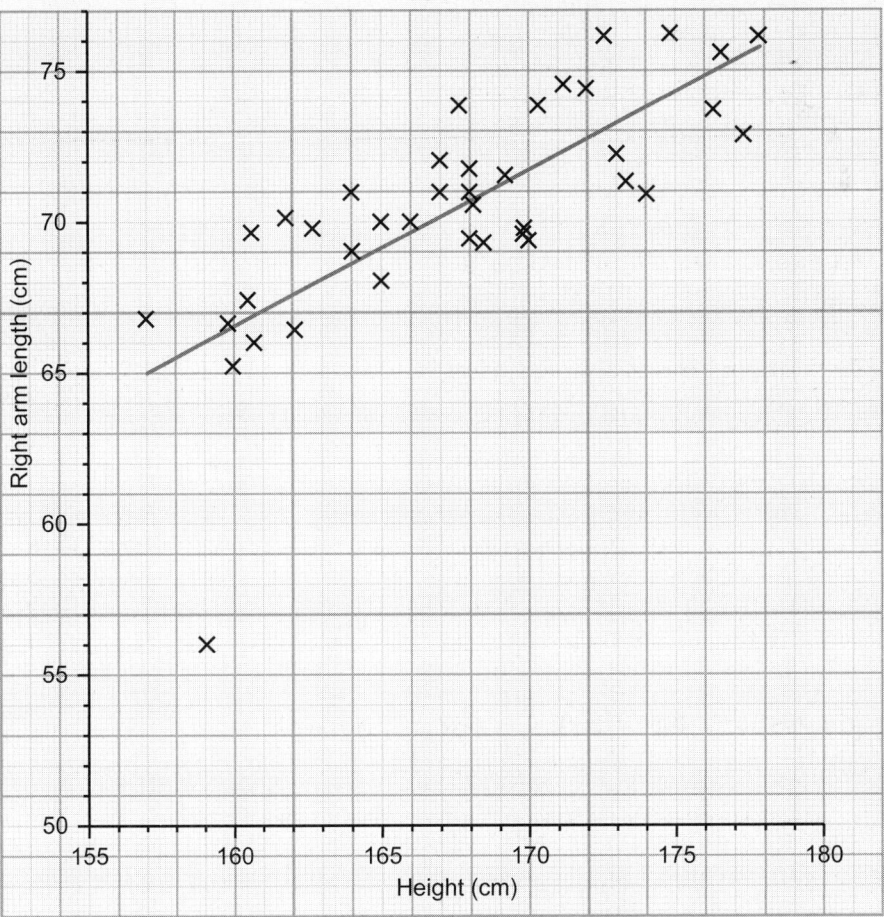

a Complete the sentence to describe the correlation shown.

Taller people have _____ .

b Circle the anomalous reading on the graph.

Practical work

You are going to measure variation in a **sample** (small selection) of people. You will use the results from your sample to look for a **relationship** in people, between their heights and their volumes of air in a normal breath.

Apparatus	Safety ⚠
• tape measure, pencil, large piece of paper, sticky tape or sticky tack • lung volume bag, mouthpiece	• Each student should use a new sterile mouthpiece or piece of tubing.

Glossary: www.pearsonschools.co.uk/KS3LabGlossary

Biology 2: Investigating variation

KS3 Science Lab Book

Planning

1 Write down the hypothesis your investigation is testing.

_____
_____

2a Write a prediction. _____

_____

b State your reasoning for your prediction. _____

_____
_____

Method 1 Measuring height

A Stick the paper to a wall, so that people's heads can rest against it.

B Take off your shoes and stand against the wall. Ask a partner to mark the top of your head on the paper.

C Measure from the floor to the mark. Record your height in centimetres (cm).

Method 2 Measuring the volume of a breath using a bag

D Hold the sealed end of the lung volume bag on a bench. Press on the sealed end of the bag with one hand and move your other hand towards the open end to push all the air out.

E Place a clean mouthpiece into the open end of the bag.

F Blow one normal breath into the bag.

G Push the air in the bag towards the sealed end. Record the volume on the scale.

H Repeat steps **D** to **G** three times. Then let others in your group follow this method, using a clean mouthpiece.

Recording your results

3a Record your results in the table below.

b Calculate the **mean** values for the volume of a breath. Add these to your table.

> **Top Tip**
> Find help on *accuracy* and means in the Appendix (sections S10 and S21).

Name	Height (cm)	Volume of a breath (cm^3)			
		1st reading	2nd reading	3rd reading	Mean

Glossary: www.pearsonschools.co.uk/KS3LabGlossary

Biology 2: Investigating variation

KS3 Science Lab Book

Considering your results / Conclusions

4 Plot the heights and mean breath volumes on a scatter graph. Put heights on the horizontal (*x*) axis. Use the grid below. Draw a line of best fit if you can.

Title: _____

> **Top Tip**
> Find help on scatter graphs in the Appendix (section S18).

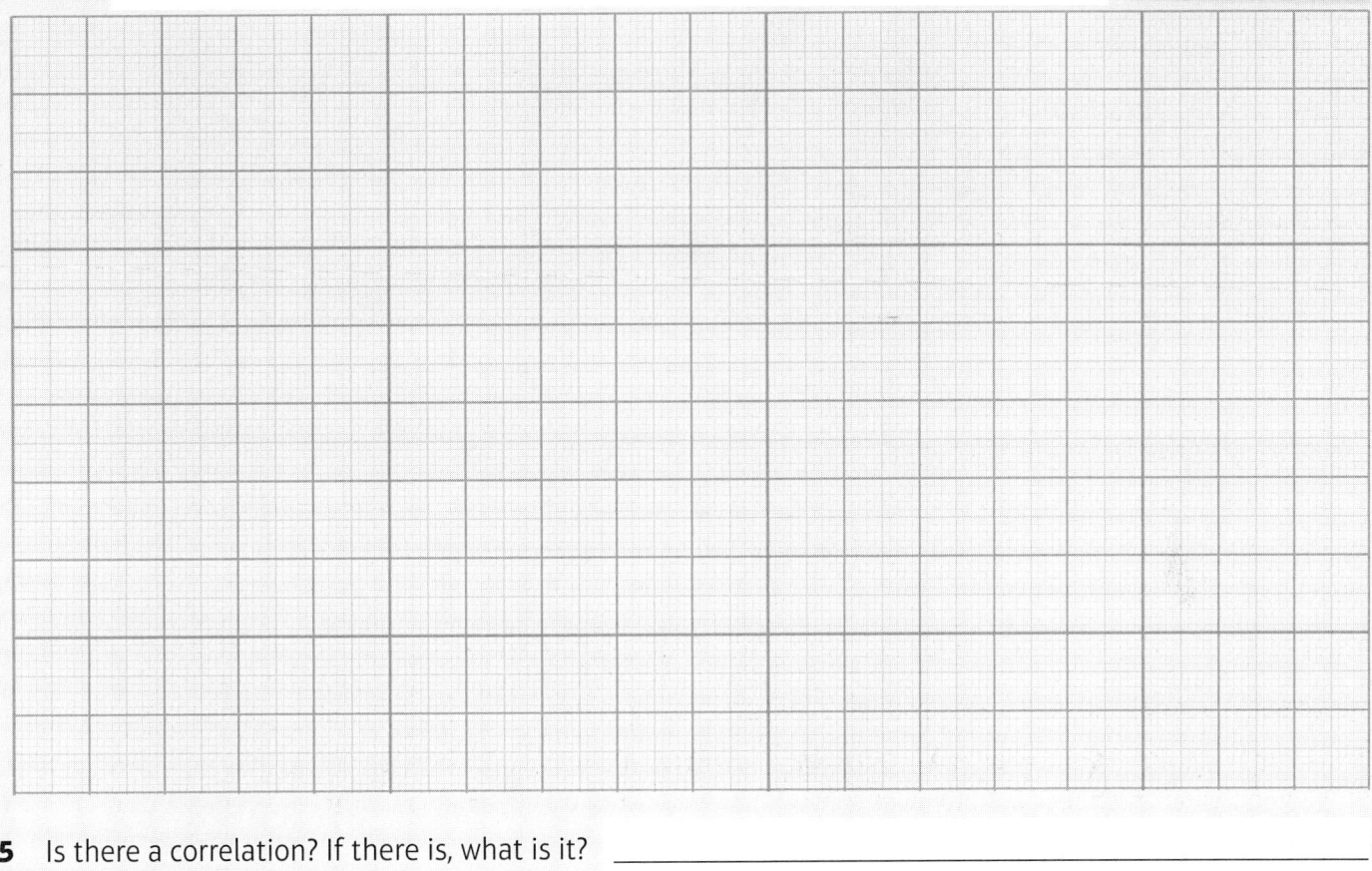

5 Is there a correlation? If there is, what is it? _____

_____

_____

6 Circle any anomalous results.

Evaluation

7a What could you do to be more certain that there is or is not a correlation?

_____

_____

_____

b The number of people in your group is your sample size. You are using your sample to look for a correlation that applies to all people. Do you think your sample size is large enough? Explain your answer.

> **Top Tip**
> Find help on samples in the Appendix (section S5).

_____

_____

Biology 2: Investigating variation

KS3 Science Lab Book

Check your understanding

1 What does each of the following describe? Answer each question using one word.

   a A description of what you think will happen in an experiment. _____

   b A factor that can change or be changed in an experiment. _____

   c A scientific idea without much **evidence**, which can be tested. _____

2 This graph shows the results of an investigation.

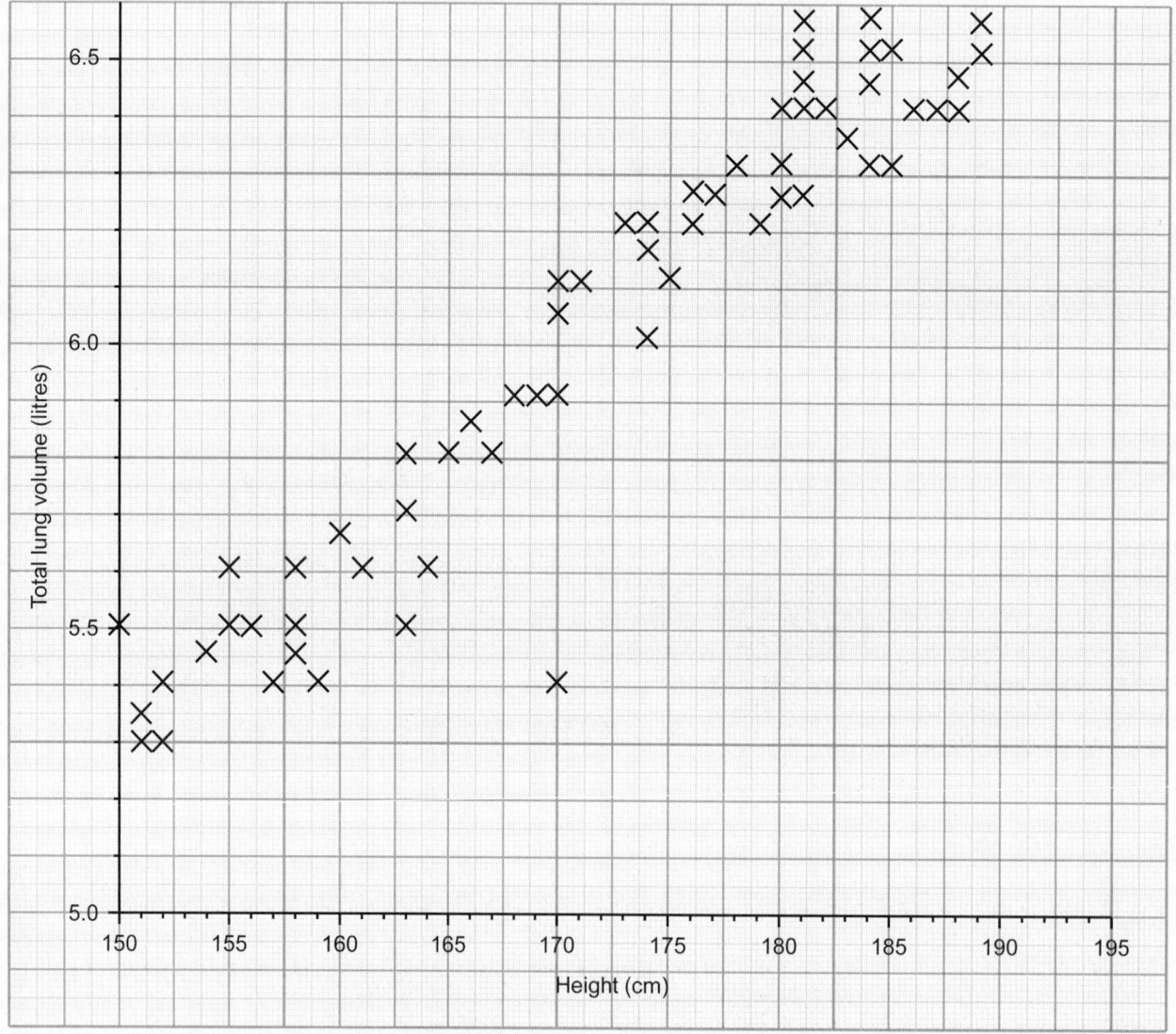

   a How do you know that there is a correlation? _____

   b Describe the correlation. _____

   c On the graph, circle the anomalous reading.

   d Draw a line of best fit through the points. Ignore the anomalous reading.

Glossary: www.pearsonschools.co.uk/KS3LabGlossary

Biology 2: Investigating variation

Checkpoint

Teacher comments

Look at the 'Skills you will develop' on page 12. In the boxes, indicate how confident you are at each skill.

What I will do to develop my skills more

Biology 3: Investigating photosynthesis

Getting started

Aim
- Find out whether chlorophyll is needed for photosynthesis.

Skills you will develop
- Describe how scientific hypotheses and theories develop.
- Identify hazards and control risks.
- Plan experiments (including making predictions).
- Draw reasoned conclusions from data.

What you need to know before starting
- ✔ Recall the main parts of a plant cell and their functions.
- ✔ Recall the reactants for and **products** of photosynthesis.

The Greek thinker Aristotle had a **hypothesis** that plants grew by consuming soil (using their roots to suck it up). In the 17th century, Belgian scientist Jan Baptista van Helmont (1580–1644) showed that the mass of soil plants used up was very small compared with the mass they gained.

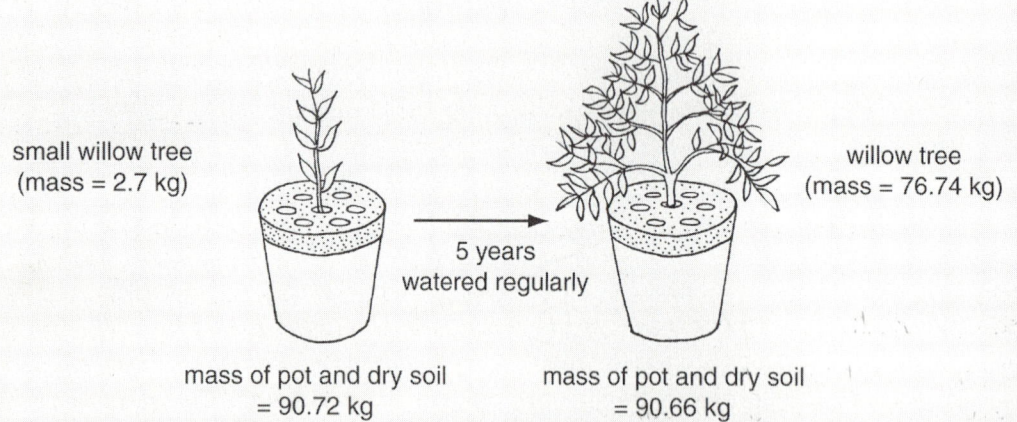

After many experiments, scientists developed a **theory** that plants make their own food using photosynthesis. We can summarise photosynthesis using a **word equation**:

carbon dioxide + water → glucose + oxygen

Top Tip
Find help on word equations in the Appendix (section S19).

Starter questions

1. How did van Helmont's **evidence** prove that Aristotle's hypothesis was wrong?

   It showed the soil only decreased by a small amount whereas the the tree grew significantly larger

Top Tip
Find help on the scientific method in the Appendix (section S2).

2. For photosynthesis, list the:

   a **reactants** *carbon dioxide, water*

   b **products.** *glucose, oxygen*

Biology 3: Investigating photosynthesis

KS3 Science Lab Book

Practical work

Plants turn the glucose they make into starch. Iodine solution is used to test for starch. It turns from a brown colour to a blue-black colour when added to starch.

Some leaves have white patches, where the cells do not contain chloroplasts (and so do not contain chlorophyll). These leaves are said to be variegated.

Apparatus
- eye protection
- variegated leaf
- ethanol
- forceps
- Petri dish
- iodine solution
- boiling tube and boiling tube holder
- large beaker
- pipette
- heat-resistant mat

Safety ⚠
- Wear eye protection.
- Take care with the beaker and the hot water; they are very hot.
- Iodine solution stains skin and may irritate your eyes.
- Ethanol is flammable.
- *wear gloves*
- _____

Top Tip
Find help on hazards and risks in the Appendix (section S4).

Planning

1a You are going to find out if chlorophyll is needed for photosynthesis. Read the method. Then tick *one* **prediction** below.
- ☐ The whole leaf will turn blue-black.
- ☑ Only the green parts of the leaf will turn blue-black.
- ☐ Only the white parts of the leaf will turn blue-black.
- ☐ No parts of the leaf will turn blue-black.

b Explain your reasoning for the prediction you have chosen.

chlorophyll gives it the green colour which also makes glucose which makes starch when iodine is added it the colour different turns

2 Read about the **hazard** of ethanol in the safety box. Add into the safety box one way of reducing the **risk** from this hazard.

Method

A Your teacher will provide you with a beaker of hot water from a kettle.

B Place the leaf in the beaker of hot water for 1 minute.

C Half-fill a boiling tube with ethanol. Place the leaf in the ethanol using forceps.

D Place the boiling tube in the beaker of hot water. Leave it for 5 minutes. Ethanol removes the green colour to make the iodine staining easier to see.

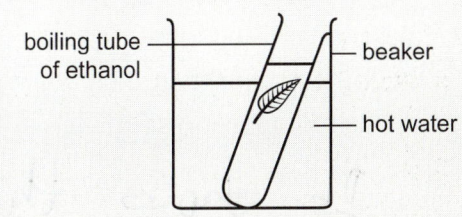

Glossary: www.pearsonschools.co.uk/KS3LabGlossary

Biology 3: Investigating photosynthesis

KS3 Science Lab Book

E   Use the forceps to take the leaf out of the boiling tube and wash it with tap water.

F   Place the leaf on a Petri dish and add five drops of iodine solution to each leaf.

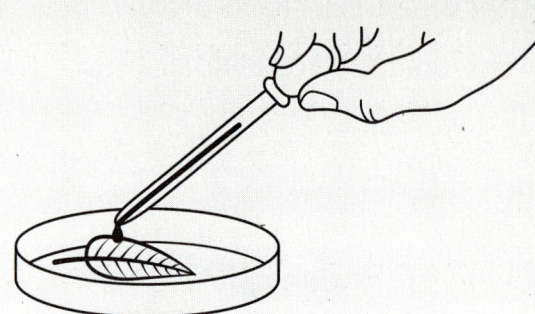

Recording your results

3   Make a labelled drawing to show which parts of your leaf turned blue-black.

Considering your results / Conclusions

4a Do your results agree with your prediction? If not, say how they differ.

Yes

b   Use your scientific knowledge to explain your findings.

I found that the leaf was kept in light because it turned blue-black which shows starch was detected it which can only be obtained from photosynthesis.

Evaluation

5   Suggest another question that could be answered by testing leaves for starch.

Was the plant kept in light or dark place

Check your understanding

1   Look at van Helmont's experiment on page 18. From this experiment, van Helmont came up with a hypothesis that the tree made its extra mass using water. How has his hypothesis been changed by other, more recent, scientists?

It shows that the soil used is less than the soil use.

Glossary: www.pearsonschools.co.uk/KS3LabGlossary

Biology 3: Investigating photosynthesis — KS3 Science Lab Book

2. While still growing on the plant, one variegated leaf had a piece of metal foil placed over it, as shown.

a Draw the leaf without the metal foil. Shade the area where you think photosynthesis occurs.

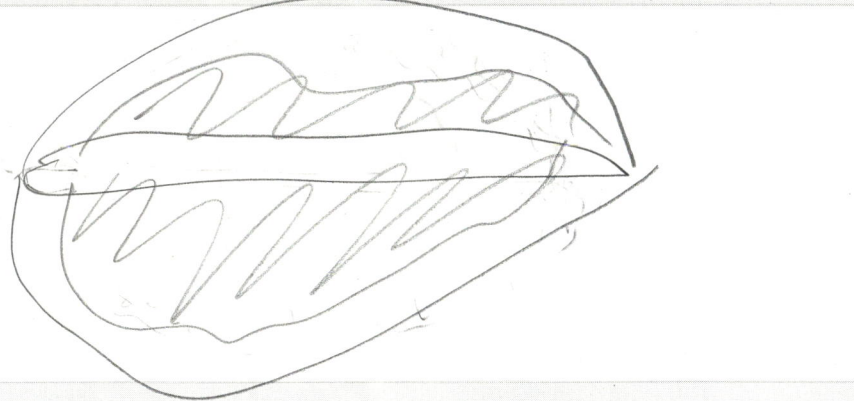

b Explain why you have shaded your leaf in this way.

The green shows that photosynthesis has occured because without starch the leaf would not be green.

Checkpoint

Teacher comments

Look at the 'Skills you will develop' on page 18. In the boxes, indicate how confident you are at each skill.

What I will do to develop my skills more

G

Biology 4: Yeast respiration

Getting started

Aim
- Test the hypothesis that the amount of carbon dioxide produced by respiring yeast depends on the temperature.

Skills you will develop
- ☐ Plan experiments to use appropriate measuring apparatus.
- ☐ Identify independent, dependent and control variables.
- ☐ Interpret and plot charts/graphs (choosing the type to use).
- ☐ Draw reasoned conclusions from data.

What you need to know before starting
✔ Explain why organisms respire.
✔ Recall what a microorganism is.

Yeast is a one-celled (unicellular) fungus. Like all organisms, yeast cells respire. They can respire aerobically (with oxygen), like humans do:

glucose + oxygen → carbon dioxide + water

If there is too little oxygen, yeast cells use **anaerobic respiration** (or **fermentation**):

glucose → carbon dioxide + ethanol

Aerobic respiration releases more energy from glucose and produces more carbon dioxide than anaerobic respiration does. Both types of respiration are a series of **chemical reactions** speeded up by **enzymes**. Many enzymes work faster when it is warm and more slowly at lower temperatures.

Starter questions

1. Explain why all organisms need to respire.

_____

_____

2. Complete the table to show how you would perform certain measurements.

Measurement	Apparatus needed	Unit of measurement	Unit symbol
mass of flour			
volume of water			
length of time			
temperature			

Biology 4: Yeast respiration

KS3 Science Lab Book

Practical work

When yeast cells respire, they produce carbon dioxide. This gas makes bread dough rise.

Apparatus
- 3 measuring cylinders
- bread flour
- dried yeast
- large beaker
- stirring rod
- sugar
- spoon
- water
- clock
- _____
- _____

Safety
- Do not eat any dough.

Prediction

1a Read the method below and then write down what you think will happen.

_____
_____

b Explain your reasoning for your **prediction**.

_____
_____
_____

2 Complete the apparatus box, adding in the missing pieces of apparatus.

Method

A Add 10 g of sugar, 3.5 g of yeast and 100 g of bread flour to a large beaker.

B Now measure out 120 cm³ of water.

C Pour the water, a little bit at a time, into the beaker. Each time you add some water, stir the **mixture** with the spoon. Keep stirring until the mixture is a smooth paste.

D Very slowly pour or spoon about 20 cm³ of the mixture into each measuring cylinder. Use a stirring rod to push down any dough that sticks to the side of the cylinder. You will not be able to add exactly 20 cm³ of dough, so record in the table the volume of dough in each cylinder.

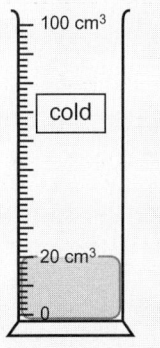
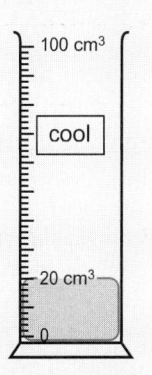
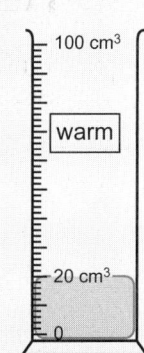

E Put the cylinders in three different places, at different temperatures. Use a thermometer to measure the exact temperature in each area.

F Leave the cylinders for 30 minutes.

G Read the new volume of dough in each cylinder.

Biology 4: Yeast respiration

KS3 Science Lab Book

Recording your results

3 Record your results in this table.

Temperature the dough was left at (°C)	Volume of dough at start (cm³)	Volume of dough at end (cm³)	Increase in dough volume (cm³)

Considering your results / Conclusions

4a State the **independent variable**. _____

b State the **dependent variable**. _____

c On the graph paper below, draw a suitable graph to look for a **relationship** between these two **variables**.

> **Top Tip**
> Find help on variables, charts and graphs in the Appendix (section S6).

Title: _____

d Is there a **correlation** between the two variables? Explain your reasoning.

_____
_____

Glossary: www.pearsonschools.co.uk/KS3LabGlossary

Biology 4: Yeast respiration

KS3 Science Lab Book

e What could you change in this experiment to be more certain of your results?

_____
_____
_____

5 State two variables that you have controlled to improve the quality of your results.

_____

6a Do your results agree with your prediction? If not, say how they differ.

_____

b Use your scientific knowledge to explain your findings.

_____
_____
_____
_____

Evaluation

7a What was the trickiest part of the experiment? _____

_____

b How do you think this might have affected your results? _____

_____
_____

c How could you improve this part of the experiment? _____

_____
_____

8 Outline a similar experiment to show that dough needs living yeast cells to make it rise.

_____
_____
_____
_____

Glossary: www.pearsonschools.co.uk/KS3LabGlossary

Biology 4: Yeast respiration

KS3 Science Lab Book

Check your understanding

1 A student mixed two bread doughs. She left 20 cm³ of each dough at a different temperature for 30 minutes. The table shows her results.

Temperature (°C)	Dough A (100 g flour, 5 g glucose, 2.5 g yeast, 120 cm³ water) Increase in dough volume (cm³)	Dough B (100 g flour, 10 g glucose, 2.5 g yeast, 120 cm³ water) Increase in dough volume (cm³)
5	10	11
20	24	30
30	33	42

a What was the final volume of dough A at 20 °C? _____

b How does temperature affect the increase in dough volume?

_____

c Explain why this happens. _____

_____

d How does the change in volume of dough B compare with that of dough A?

_____

e Complete the sentence to explain the difference in the change in volume.

Dough B contains more _____ and so more _____ occurs,

which means that more _____ is produced.

Checkpoint

Teacher comments

Look at the 'Skills you will develop' on page 22. In the boxes, indicate how confident you are at each skill.
What I will do to develop my skills more

Chemistry 1: Testing indigestion remedies

KS3 Science Lab Book

Getting started

Aim
- Test a range of indigestion remedies to decide which is best at neutralising acids.

Skills you will develop
- ☐ Identify hazards and control risks.
- ☐ Identify independent, dependent and control variables.
- ☐ Use systematic tables to record observations and data.

What you need to know before starting

✔ Recall the meanings of the terms acid, alkali, base, indicator, insoluble, neutralisation, pH, soluble.

Acids and alkalis are common substances. Some are **corrosive**, which means they can attack various materials (such as metals or skin). Corrosive substances are **hazards**, which means they can cause harm. In the lab, we usually dilute acids and alkalis with water to reduce the **risk** of harm from them. Dilute acids and alkalis can still cause harm, though, and need to be handled with care.

Starter questions

1 Draw lines to join the correct sentence halves together.

An acid …	… neutralises an acid, to form a salt and water.
An alkali …	… dissolves.
A base …	… turns litmus red.
An indicator …	… is a soluble base.
An insoluble substance …	… does not dissolve.
Neutralisation …	… changes colour in solutions of different acidity.
pH …	… is a type of reaction between an acid and a base.
A soluble substance …	… is a scale showing how acidic or alkaline a solution is.

2 The **concentration** of a solution is the mass of **solute** dissolved in a certain volume. For example, a sugar solution that contains 2 g of sugar dissolved in each 1 cm^3 of water (2 g/cm^3) is more concentrated than a 1 g/cm^3 sugar solution.

   a Which of the following sugar solutions is the most concentrated? Circle your answer.

   1 g/1 cm^3 0.2 g/1 cm^3 10 g/10 cm^3 0.5 g/1 cm^3 1.5 g/1 cm^3

   b Explain how you made your choice. _____

   _____

   _____

3 **Hazard symbols** warn you about substances that may cause harm. Circle the hazard symbol below that means 'Caution: this substance may cause skin irritation.'

Top Tip

Find help on hazard symbols in the Appendix (section S4).

Chemistry 1: Testing indigestion remedies

4 A student has three concentrations of an acid (X, Y and Z). They want to discover how much of an insoluble base neutralises 100 cm³ of each acid (to form a solution of pH 7). The table shows the results.

Acid	Mass of base needed to neutralise (g)
X	5
Y	20
Z	17

> **Top Tip**
> Find help on variables in the Appendix (section S6).

a Label the table to show which column shows the **dependent variable** and which shows the **independent variable**.

b Which acid was the most concentrated? _____

c Explain how you know this. _____

d We try to keep some **variables** the same. These are called **control variables**. State two control variables in this experiment. _____

e What chemical test would you use to discover the pH of a solution? _____

5 Magnesium chloride and water are formed when magnesium hydroxide solution is mixed with hydrochloric acid. Write a **word equation** for this neutralisation reaction.

> **Top Tip**
> Find help on word equations in the Appendix (section S19).

Chemistry 1: Testing indigestion remedies

KS3 Science Lab Book

Practical work

Too much hydrochloric acid in your stomach can give you indigestion pains. Remedies for indigestion (often called antacids) contain a base, such as magnesium hydroxide.

Apparatus
- eye protection
- 5 large test tubes
- test-tube rack
- measuring cylinder
- 4 small samples of indigestion remedies
- stirring rod
- universal indicator paper and colour chart
- dilute hydrochloric acid

Safety
- Dilute acids can irritate eyes – wear eye protection.

Planning

1 Look at the apparatus and safety information.

   a State one hazard. _____

   b State how you will reduce the risk of this hazard causing harm. _____

   _____

> **Top Tip**
> Find help on hazards and risks in the Appendix (section S4).

Method

A Measure out 10 cm³ of acid into each test tube. Stand the tubes in the rack.

B Drop a piece of pH paper into the first test tube. Record its colour and pH number.

C Add the first antacid **sample** to the second test tube containing acid. Use all of the sample and record the name of the indigestion remedy in the results table.

D Stir the **mixture** in the test tube. Rinse the stirring rod.

E After 2 minutes, drop a piece of pH paper into the test tube. Record the colour and pH number and describe what the mixture looks like.

F Repeat steps **C** to **E** with the other samples and test tubes. Record your results in the table.

Recording your results

2 Record your results in the table below.

Remedy	Name (if any)	Colour of pH paper	pH	Appearance
None				
1				
2				
3				
4				

Glossary: www.pearsonschools.co.uk/KS3LabGlossary

Chemistry 1: Testing indigestion remedies

KS3 Science Lab Book

Considering your results / Conclusions

3a What was the independent variable in this experiment? _____

b What was the dependent variable? _____

c State one of the control variables. _____

4 State the name of the reaction that increases the pH in the tubes. _____

5 In which test tubes was the acid neutralised? _____

6 Which test tubes were cloudy at the end? _____

7 Which remedy do you think is best? Explain your answer. _____

_____

_____

Check your understanding

Two students were each given four powdered indigestion remedies. They planned to discover the best remedy. Read the plans and answer the questions by circling the letters.

Student A's plan

I will put 20 cm³ of dilute hydrochloric acid in a beaker and add a spatula of a powder. I will test the liquid with universal indicator paper. I will add more powder until it changes to pH 7. I will count how many spatulas of powder I need. I will repeat this for each remedy.

Student B's plan

A Half fill four test tubes with dilute hydrochloric acid.
B Add two spatulas of a different indigestion remedy to each one.
C Measure the pH in each tube.

1 What type of chemical reaction occurs when a base is mixed with an acid? ☐ **A** decomposition ☐ **B** neutralisation ☐ **C** acidification ☐ **D** combustion	2 What is a control variable in both plans? ☐ **A** pH ☐ **B** amount of powder added ☐ **C** type of indigestion remedy ☐ **D** volume of acid
	3 What is the independent variable in both plans? ☐ **A** pH ☐ **B** amount of powder added ☐ **C** type of indigestion remedy ☐ **D** volume of acid

Glossary: www.pearsonschools.co.uk/KS3LabGlossary

Chemistry 1: Testing indigestion remedies

4 Which hazard symbol is most likely to be found on the acid bottle that the students use?

- [ ] A
- [ ] B
- [ ] C
- [ ] D

5 What is Student B's dependent variable?
- [ ] A pH
- [ ] B amount of powder added
- [ ] C type of indigestion remedy
- [ ] D volume of acid

6 What is Student A's dependent variable?
- [ ] A pH
- [ ] B amount of powder added
- [ ] C type of indigestion remedy
- [ ] D volume of acid

Checkpoint

Teacher comments

Look at the 'Skills you will develop' on page 27. In the boxes, indicate how confident you are at each skill.

What I will do to develop my skills more

Glossary: www.pearsonschools.co.uk/KS3LabGlossary

Chemistry 2: Separating mixtures

KS3 Science Lab Book

Getting started

Aims
- Separate common salt from rock salt.
- Separate the colours in ink.

Skills you will develop
- ☐ Identify hazards and control risks.
- ☐ Set up and use a Bunsen burner safely.
- ☐ Separate mixtures using appropriate techniques.
- ☐ Produce labelled drawings and diagrams (of glassware).

What you need to know before starting
✔ Describe how to use a Bunsen burner safely.
✔ Describe how to carry out filtration.
✔ Explain what happens to a solution during evaporation.
✔ Explain what happens during simple chromatography.
✔ Recall the meanings of the terms: evaporation, filter, filtrate, filtration, insoluble, soluble, solute, solution, solvent.

A **mixture** is two or more substances jumbled up together but not joined to one another. The substances in a mixture can often be separated.

Starter questions

1 Use an appropriate colour pencil to add the flame to each of these Bunsen burner drawings. Remember to draw the correct size of flame, as well as the correct colour.

a flame for heating strongly   **b** flame for gentle heating   **c** safety flame

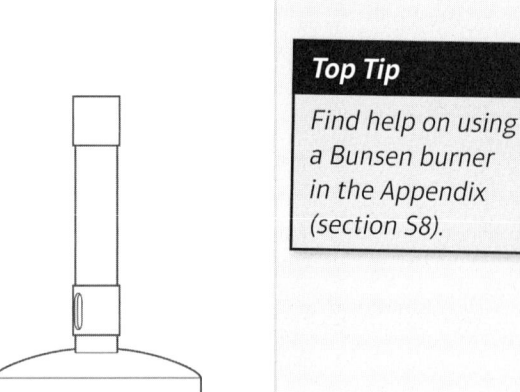

Top Tip

Find help on using a Bunsen burner in the Appendix (section S8).

2a Describe one **hazard** of heating with a Bunsen burner.

_____

Glossary: www.pearsonschools.co.uk/KS3LabGlossary

Chemistry 2: Separating mixtures

b Describe one way that you could reduce the **risk** of being harmed by this hazard.

> **Top Tip**
> Find help on hazards and risks in the Appendix (section S4).

Practical work

Rock salt is a mixture of rock and salt. Inks are also mixtures and may contain many different coloured pigments. You are going to try to separate the components of both these mixtures.

Experiment 1 Separating salt from rock salt

Apparatus	Safety
• eye protection • rock salt • mortar and pestle • evaporating basin • filter funnels and papers • beaker • conical flask • stirring rod • measuring cylinder • heating apparatus (Bunsen burner, heat-resistant mat, tripod, gauze) • electronic balance • water	• Wear eye protection. • Heat the evaporating basin with a medium flame and **do not** heat the salt solution to dryness; hot specks of salt will spit out. • Stop heating when crystals start to form. Let the remaining water evaporate without heating. • Do not touch the hot evaporating basin. • Use a safety flame when the Bunsen burner is not in use and before turning off. • Wash your hands afterwards.

Method

1a Letter the statements in the method on the following page to show the correct order. Use the letters **A** to **J**.

b Add labels to the diagrams. The words you need are below. You may use each word once, more than once or not at all.

| beaker | bits of rock | conical flask | evaporating basin | funnel | heat |
| pestle | pure salt | rock salt | salty water | stirring rod | tripod |

> **Top Tip**
> Find help on pieces of apparatus in the Appendix (section S11).

Chemistry 2: Separating mixtures

KS3 Science Lab Book

- ☐ Filter the mixture, using a funnel and filter paper. Use a conical flask to collect the filtrate.
- ☐ You may be given a sample of rock salt or asked to measure a certain mass. Crush it using a mortar and pestle.
- ☐ The insoluble bits of rock will be trapped in the filter paper. Salty water will pass through the filter paper.
- ☐ Evaporate the filtrate in an evaporating basin. Heat *gently*.
- ☐ Put the crushed-up rock salt into a beaker and add 50 cm³ of water.
- ☐ This releases any salt trapped inside bits of rock and makes dissolving the lumps of salt quicker.
- ☐ The salt is soluble and will dissolve. The bits of rock are insoluble.
- ☐ The water evaporates and leaves the salt behind.
- ☐ The filtrate contains the salt. The filter paper does not trap the salt because the salt is dissolved in the water.
- ☐ Stir the mixture.

2 Filtration is not shown. In the space below, draw a labelled diagram of the mixture being filtered.

Top Tip

Find help on drawing apparatus in the Appendix (section S11).

3a Describe the hazard from the evaporating basin when it has been heated.

b How will you reduce the risk of harm from this hazard?

Top Tip

Find help on hazards and risks in the Appendix (section S4).

Glossary: www.pearsonschools.co.uk/KS3LabGlossary

Chemistry 2: Separating mixtures

KS3 Science Lab Book

c Describe the hazard from the salt in the evaporating basin if you heat it for too long.

d How will you reduce the risk of harm from this hazard?

Once your teacher has checked your work, you may be asked to do the practical.

Recording your results

4 Describe a difference between the rock salt and the evaporated filtrate

Considering your results / Conclusions

5 What properties of common salt and rock allow them to be separated in this way?

Experiment 2 Separating substances in inks

Apparatus	Safety
• coloured ink(s) or felt pens or other coloured substances • chromatography paper or filter paper • beaker • water • paper clips • pipette/dropper • pencil and ruler	• Tell your teacher if you spill any ink.

Chromatography can separate a mixture of soluble substances that dissolve in the same **solvent**. In paper chromatography, the solvent (usually water) travels through paper and carries the soluble substances with it. However, these substances travel at different **speeds** and so end up at different distances from the starting line on the **chromatogram**.

Method

A Using a pencil, draw a straight line across the filter paper, 2 cm from the bottom. Draw *one* pencil cross on the line for each chemical you want to investigate, and number the crosses. Your paper should look like this.

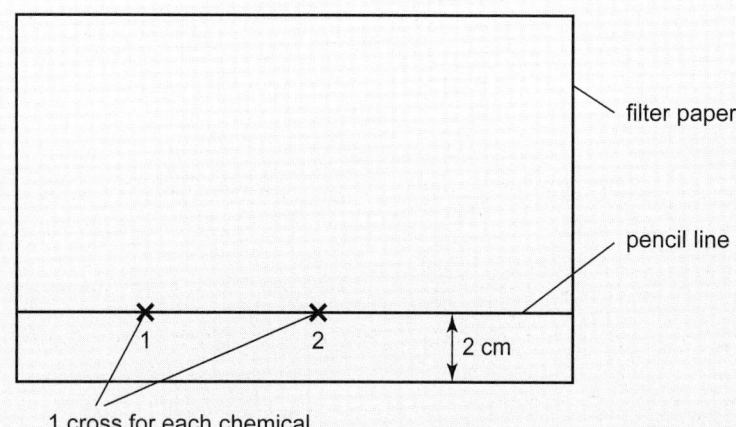

Glossary: www.pearsonschools.co.uk/KS3LabGlossary

Chemistry 2: Separating mixtures

B Place a *small* dot of ink on one cross. When it is dry, add a second small dot of the same ink on top of the first one. Record which ink you are testing on each numbered cross.

C Repeat step **B** for the other inks on the other crosses.

D Put about 1 cm depth of water in the bottom of the large beaker.

E When the ink spots have dried, roll up the paper and clip it with paper clips. Place it into the beaker, with the dots at the bottom. The ink dots should *not* be in the water.

F Leave the water to soak up the paper until the water has nearly reached the top. Remove the filter paper from the beaker and hang it up to dry.

Recording your results

1   Draw a picture of your chromatogram below, or stick in the dry chromatogram.

Chemistry 3: Investigating chemical reactions

KS3 Science Lab Book

Getting started

Aim
- Investigate the changes in mass when copper carbonate and magnesium are heated.

Skills you will develop
- ☐ Use models (word equations).
- ☐ Set up and use a Bunsen burner safely.
- ☐ Draw reasoned conclusions from data.
- ☐ Present data to a certain degree of accuracy (masses to 2 decimal places).
- ☐ Perform calculations.

What you need to know before starting

✔ Describe how all materials are made of particles.
✔ Recall the names of some common gases in the air.
✔ Recall the difference between a chemical reaction and a physical change.
✔ Recall the difference between an element and a compound.

In a **chemical reaction**, the particles of one or more substances (the **reactants**) are rearranged. This process forms new substances (the **products**). The total number of particles does not change, and so the mass of the reactants equals the mass of the products. A **word equation** is a **model** showing what happens in a chemical reaction.

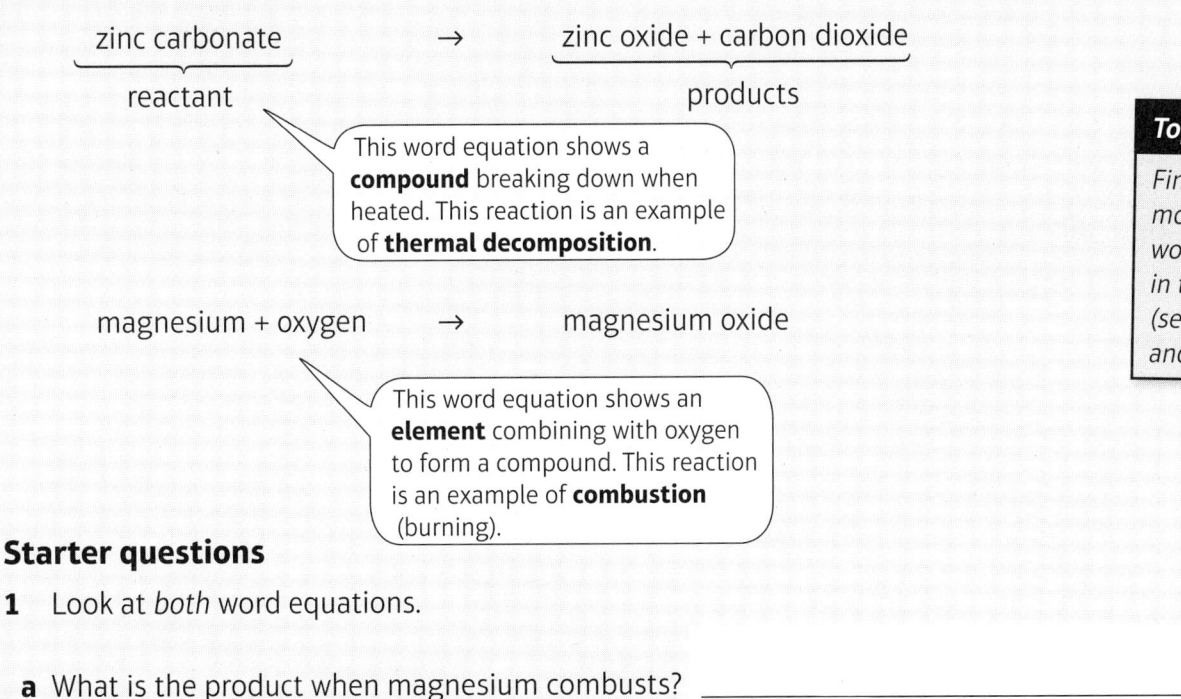

zinc carbonate → zinc oxide + carbon dioxide
  reactant   products

This word equation shows a **compound** breaking down when heated. This reaction is an example of **thermal decomposition**.

magnesium + oxygen → magnesium oxide

This word equation shows an **element** combining with oxygen to form a compound. This reaction is an example of **combustion** (burning).

Top Tip

Find help on models and word equations in the Appendix (sections S1 and S19).

Starter questions

1 Look at *both* word equations.

   a What is the product when magnesium combusts? _____

   b What are the products of the thermal decomposition of zinc carbonate?
   _____

   c Name one reactant that is a compound. _____

   d Name one product that is a gas. _____

   e List the reactants that are **elements**. _____

Glossary: www.pearsonschools.co.uk/KS3LabGlossary

Chemistry 3: Investigating chemical reactions

KS3 Science Lab Book

Practical work

You will measure the changes in mass during some chemical reactions. The investigation is divided into two parts. In the first part you will investigate heating copper carbonate. In the second part you will investigate the **combustion** of magnesium.

Experiment 1 Heating copper carbonate

Apparatus
- eye protection
- Bunsen burner
- heat-resistant mat
- clamp and stand or test-tube holder
- test tube
- balance
- spatula
- copper carbonate

Safety
- Wear eye protection.
- When heating the copper carbonate, make sure that the open end of your test tube is not pointing towards anyone.
- Wash your hands after this experiment.
- Take care if you are asthmatic.

Prediction

1a In the space below, write a word equation for what happens when copper carbonate is heated.

Top Tip
The reaction is similar to when zinc carbonate is heated.

b Predict what you think will happen to the mass of the powder as it is heated.

c Explain your reasoning for your **prediction**.

Method

A Measure the mass of a test tube. Record the mass to two **decimal places** (two numbers after the decimal point). Make sure you set the balance to zero before measuring the mass.

B Add three spatulas of copper carbonate to the tube.

C Measure the mass of the test tube again. Record the mass to two decimal places.

D Hold your tube above a Bunsen burner as shown.

E Heat the tube using a medium flame for 2 minutes and then use a roaring flame.

F Stop heating when all the copper carbonate has changed colour.

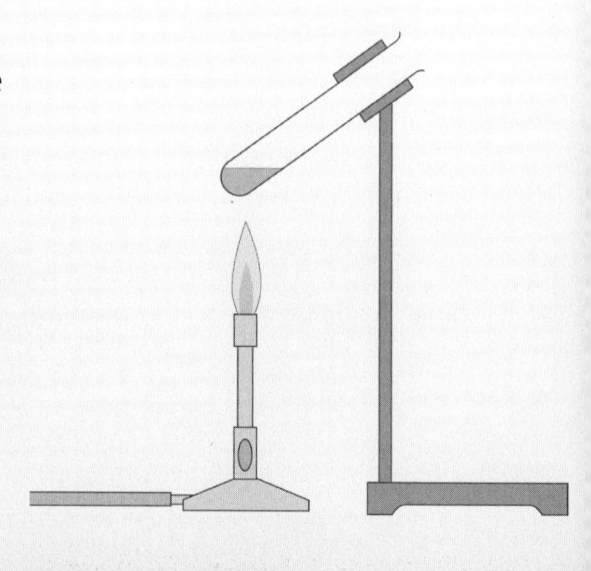

Glossary: www.pearsonschools.co.uk/KS3LabGlossary

Chemistry 3: Investigating chemical reactions

KS3 Science Lab Book

G Turn off the Bunsen burner and allow everything to cool for 10 minutes.

H Measure the mass of the test tube and product. Record the mass to two decimal places.

Recording your results

2 Record your readings in the table below.

Step A Mass of empty test tube (g)	Step C Mass of test tube + reactant (g)	Mass of reactant (g)	Step H Mass of test tube after heating (g)	Mass of product (g)

3 Describe how you could tell that a chemical reaction was occurring.

_____

_____

Considering your results / Conclusions

4a In the mathematical **equation** below, fill in your readings from step **A** and step **C**. Then calculate the mass of copper carbonate (the reactant).

(Mass of test tube + copper carbonate) – mass of empty test tube   =   mass of reactant

_____   _____   _____

Mass of reactant = _____

b Calculate the mass of the product. Show your working.

> **Top Tip**
> Use your readings from step A and step H.

Mass of product = _____

c Calculate the change in mass during the reaction. Show your working.

> **Top Tip**
> Use your answers to part **a** and part **b**. A positive number shows an increase in mass. A negative number shows a decrease in mass.

Change in mass = _____

5a Do your results agree with your prediction? If not, say how they differ. _____

_____

Glossary: www.pearsonschools.co.uk/KS3LabGlossary

Chemistry 3: Investigating chemical reactions

b Use your scientific knowledge to explain the change in mass in this reaction.

___

Experiment 2 Heating magnesium

Apparatus		Safety
• eye protection • magnesium ribbon • pipe clay triangle • Bunsen burner • balance	• heat-resistant mat • tongs • crucible with lid • tripod • emery paper	• Wear eye protection. • Use tongs to handle apparatus, as it will take time to cool down after heating. • Do not look directly at burning magnesium. • Wash your hands after this experiment.

Prediction

1 You will investigate the change in mass of magnesium ribbon when heated.

a Predict what you think will happen to the mass of the magnesium as it is heated.

___

b Explain your reasoning for your prediction.

___

Method

A If the magnesium looks dull or black, rub it with emery paper until it is shiny.

B Measure the mass of the crucible and lid. Record the mass to 2 decimal places.

C Wrap the magnesium ribbon into a loose coil and put it in the crucible. Measure the mass of the crucible, lid and magnesium. Record the mass to 2 decimal places.

D Set up the apparatus as shown. Ensure the crucible is secure and the lid is fully on.

E Light the Bunsen burner and use a roaring flame to heat the crucible.

F Once the magnesium starts to burn, use the tongs to lift the lid slightly to let in air. Do not allow the flame from the magnesium to escape, as this allows product to escape.

G Keep heating and lifting the lid until you see no further reaction. Use the tongs to remove the crucible lid and place it on the heat-resistant mat. Heat for another 2 minutes.

H Turn off the Bunsen burner and allow everything to cool for 5 minutes.

I Measure the mass of the crucible, lid and product. Record the mass to 2 decimal places.

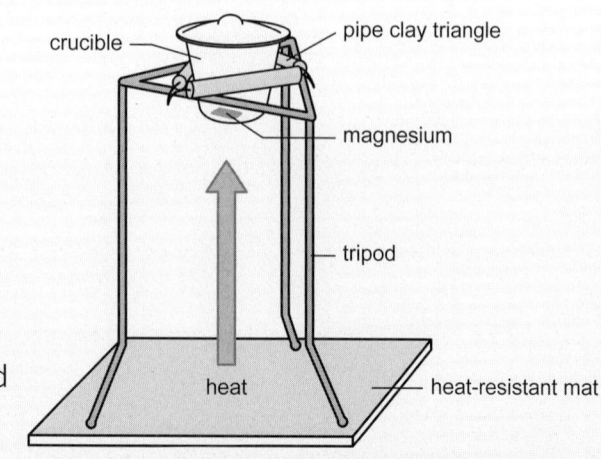

Glossary: www.pearsonschools.co.uk/KS3LabGlossary

Chemistry 3: Investigating chemical reactions

KS3 Science Lab Book

Recording your results

2 Record your readings in the table below.

Mass of crucible + lid (g)	Mass of crucible + lid + reactant (g)	Mass of reactant (g)	Mass of crucible + lid + product (g)	Mass of product (g)

3 Describe how you could tell that a chemical reaction was occurring.

_____

_____

Considering your results / Conclusions

4a Calculate the mass of magnesium used. Show your working.

Mass of magnesium = _____

b Calculate the mass of the product. Show your working.

Mass of product = _____

c Calculate the change in mass during the reaction. Show your working.

> **Top Tip**
> Use your answers to part **a** and part **b**. A positive number shows an increase in mass. A negative number shows a decrease in mass.

Change in mass = _____

5a Do your results agree with your prediction? If not, say how they differ. _____

_____

b Use your scientific knowledge to explain the change in mass in this reaction.

_____

_____

_____

Glossary: www.pearsonschools.co.uk/KS3LabGlossary

Chemistry 3: Investigating chemical reactions

KS3 Science Lab Book

Evaluation

6 This experiment does not often give **accurate** values for the change in mass. If you repeat the experiment with the same mass of magnesium, you are unlikely to get the same result. Three reasons for this are given below. Reason **a** has been explained. Complete the explanation for Reasons **b** and **c**.

a Reason: Some product escapes when you lift the lid.

Effect: *Change in mass is below the true value.*

Explanation: *There will be less product. So, the final mass measurement will be too low. This makes the change in mass value lower than its true value.*

b Reason: Not all the magnesium reacts.

Effect: _____

Explanation: _____

_____

_____

c Reason: The balance was not zeroed and it showed a positive value before the crucible and lid were put on it.

Effect: _____

Explanation: _____

_____

_____

Check your understanding

1 Some scientists heated some calcium in air to investigate the change in mass when it combusts. The only product was calcium oxide. The table shows all their readings.

Mass of crucible + lid (g)	Mass of crucible + lid + reactant (g)	Mass of reactant (g)	Mass of crucible + lid + product (g)	Mass of product (g)
19.33	22.45		23.72	

a Complete the table. Show your working in the space below.

Glossary: www.pearsonschools.co.uk/KS3LabGlossary

Chemistry 3: Investigating chemical reactions

KS3 Science Lab Book

b Calculate the change in mass during the reaction. Show your working.

Change in mass = _____

c Write a word equation for this reaction.

d Explain why the product has a greater mass than the reactant.

_____

_____

3 When wood combusts, carbon dioxide and water are formed, and a solid 'ash' is left. Eighteenth-century scientists thought that substances contained phlogiston ('*flo-**jist**-on*'). According to this **theory**, phlogiston escaped when substances burned, leaving ash. This explained why wood lost mass when burned. In the 1770s, Antoine Lavoisier and Joseph Priestley showed that the theory was wrong. They identified the gas products of some reactions, and found that their mass matched the mass lost by the reactants.

After wood has combusted, the ash left behind has a smaller mass than the original wood. Compare how the phlogiston theory and our current theory explain this.

_____

_____

_____

_____

Checkpoint

Teacher comments

Look at the 'Skills you will develop' on page 39. In the boxes, indicate how confident you are at each skill.

What I will do to develop my skills more

Chemistry 4: Energy and reactions

KS3 Science Lab Book

Getting started

Aim
- Classify some reactions as exothermic or endothermic.

Skills you will develop
- ☐ Plan experiments.
- ☐ Use systematic tables to record observations and data.
- ☐ Interpret and plot charts/graphs (bar charts, scatter graphs, lines of best fit).
- ☐ Suggest ways to improve an experiment.

What you need to know before starting
- ✔ Measure temperatures and volumes accurately.
- ✔ Describe how to use a Bunsen burner safely.
- ✔ Describe how energy is conducted better through some materials than others.
- ✔ Recall the meanings of the terms: chemical reaction, combustion, reactant, product.

Energy cannot be created or destroyed. It can only be transferred or stored.

A **chemical reaction** in which energy stored in the **reactants** is transferred to the surroundings is an **exothermic reaction**. In the surroundings, the addition of energy causes the temperature to increase.

A reaction in which energy is transferred from the surroundings to the reactants is an **endothermic reaction**. In the surroundings, the removal of energy lowers the temperature.

Starter questions

1a Describe the safety flame of a Bunsen burner. _____

b When would you use a safety flame? _____

c What position should the air hole be in to produce a safety flame? _____

d Describe the flame used to heat things strongly. _____

e In a Bunsen burner, a chemical reaction occurs in which the fuel is burnt. What is the scientific term for this type of reaction? Tick *one* box.
- ☐ thermal decomposition
- ☐ neutralisation
- ☐ combustion
- ☐ displacement

2 Ammonium nitrate is added to water.

Start temperature = 20 °C

End temperature = 15 °C

Complete the sentence below by selecting words from the box.

| decreased   dissolving   endothermic   exothermic   increased |

This process is _____ because the temperature of the surroundings _____ .

Glossary: www.pearsonschools.co.uk/KS3LabGlossary

Chemistry 4: Energy and reactions

KS3 Science Lab Book

Practical work

You will measure how the temperature of the surroundings changes during some chemical reactions. The investigation is divided into two parts. In the first part you will investigate the **combustion** of natural gas in a Bunsen burner. In the second part you will investigate some other reactions.

Experiment 1 Burning natural gas

Aim
- Investigate how the temperature of 220 cm^3 of water changes over time as you heat it using a Bunsen burner.

> **Top Tip**
> Find help on using a Bunsen burner in the Appendix (section S8).

Prediction
1. Write a list of all the apparatus you will need for this investigation.

Apparatus	Safety ⚠
	• Wear eye protection. • Move the Bunsen burner using its base. • Do not heat your water above 80 °C.

Method
2. Plan your investigation.

   a What is your **independent variable**? _____

   b What is your **dependent variable**? _____

> **Top Tip**
> Find help on **variables** in the Appendix (section S6).

3a Read the information above and then write a step-by-step plan. Label each step with a letter. Decide how many readings you will make. Make sure your plan follows the guidance in the safety box.

_____
_____
_____
_____
_____
_____

Glossary: www.pearsonschools.co.uk/KS3LabGlossary

Chemistry 4: Energy and reactions

b In the space below, draw a diagram of your set-up.

Top Tip
Find help on drawing apparatus in the Appendix (section S11).

Get your method approved by your teacher before you start practical work.

Recording your results

4 Carry out your planned experiment. Record your readings in a table. Use the grid below to draw a neat table.

Top Tip
Find help on tables in the Appendix (section S13).

Chemistry 4: Energy and reactions

KS3 Science Lab Book

Considering your results / Conclusions

5 On the graph paper below, draw a **scatter graph** to see whether there is a **correlation** between the length of heating time and the temperature.

> **Top Tip**
> Find help on correlations and scatter graphs in the Appendix (sections S23 and S18).

Title: _____

_____

_____

6a Describe any correlation you can see in your graph. _____

_____

b Use your scientific knowledge to explain the correlation.

_____

_____

Evaluation

7 Use your graph to **estimate** the temperature of the water at the following times.

a 90 seconds _____

b 2 minutes and 30 seconds _____

c 3 minutes and 40 seconds _____

8 State and explain one way in which this experiment might be improved.

> **Top Tip**
> Find help on evaluating in the Appendix (section S25).

_____

_____

Glossary: www.pearsonschools.co.uk/KS3LabGlossary

Chemistry 4: Energy and reactions

KS3 Science Lab Book

9 Methane and butane are both used as fuels. Outline how you could use this experiment (Experiment 1) to find out which gas – methane or butane – stores more energy. Describe how you would use the results to give you an answer.

_____

_____

_____

_____

_____

Experiment 2 Energy changes in other reactions

Apparatus	Safety
• polystyrene cup supported in a beaker • thermometer • 25 cm³ measuring cylinder • watch glass • spatula • hydrochloric acid • sodium hydroxide solution • copper sulfate solution • zinc powder • ammonium chloride • distilled or de-ionised water • goggles • stirring rod	• Sodium hydroxide solution is corrosive. • Wear goggles (chemical splash-proof). • Zinc is highly flammable and a danger to the environment. • Do not tip metal residues down the sink. • Take care – some chemicals are irritants and some may be corrosive to your eyes.

Method

Reaction 1

A Place 25 cm³ of dilute hydrochloric acid into the polystyrene cup supported in the beaker.

B Measure the temperature of the hydrochloric acid and record it in the table below.

C Rinse the measuring cylinder with water.

D Measure out 25 cm³ of sodium hydroxide solution.

E Add the sodium hydroxide to the acid and stir the **mixture** with the stirring rod.

F Record the highest or lowest temperature reached (i.e. the final temperature).

Reaction 2

A Rinse and dry the polystyrene cup.

B Rinse the measuring cylinder.

C Place 25 cm³ of distilled or de-ionised water into the polystyrene cup. Place the polystyrene cup in a beaker to support it.

D Record the temperature of the water.

E Put two spatulas of ammonium chloride on the watch glass.

F Add the ammonium chloride to the water and stir the mixture with the stirring rod.

G Record the highest or lowest temperature reached.

Glossary: www.pearsonschools.co.uk/KS3LabGlossary

Chemistry 4: Energy and reactions

KS3 Science Lab Book

Reaction 3

A Rinse and dry the polystyrene cup and watch glass.
B Rinse the measuring cylinder.
C Place 25 cm^3 of copper sulfate solution into the polystyrene cup supported in the beaker.
D Record the temperature of the copper sulfate solution.
E Put two spatulas of zinc powder on the watch glass.
F Add the zinc to the copper sulfate solution and stir the mixture with the stirring rod.
G Record the highest or lowest temperature reached.

Recording your results

1 Record your readings in the table below.

Reaction	Starting temperature (°C)	Final temperature (°C)	Temperature change (°C)	Exothermic or endothermic
1				
2				
3				

Considering your results / Conclusions

2 Calculate the temperature change for each reaction and record it in the table. Include a + sign if the temperature of the surroundings increased or a − sign if the temperature of the surroundings decreased.

3 Use the temperature changes to decide whether an exothermic or an endothermic reaction took place.

Evaluation

4 Explain why you used a polystyrene cup for these reactions instead of a glass beaker.

_____

_____

_____

5 Explain why it was important to stir the reaction mixtures.

_____

_____

_____

6 Suggest what you could do to these reactions to increase the temperature changes.

_____

_____

Glossary: www.pearsonschools.co.uk/KS3LabGlossary

Chemistry 4: Energy and reactions

Check your understanding

1. The table below shows some **data** about some chemical reactions. The initial and final temperatures were measured for each reaction.

Reactants	Start temperature /°C	End temperature /°C	Temperature change /°C	Exothermic or endothermic
hydrochloric acid and sodium hydroxide	18	30		
ethanoic acid and sodium carbonate	18	12		
magnesium and copper sulfate solution	18	65		
ammonium nitrate and water	18	15		

   a Calculate the temperature change for each reaction and record it in the table. Include a + sign or – sign to show whether the temperature increased (+) or decreased (–).

   b Deduce whether each reaction was exothermic or endothermic and complete the table.

   c On the graph paper, plot a suitable **bar chart** to show the results.

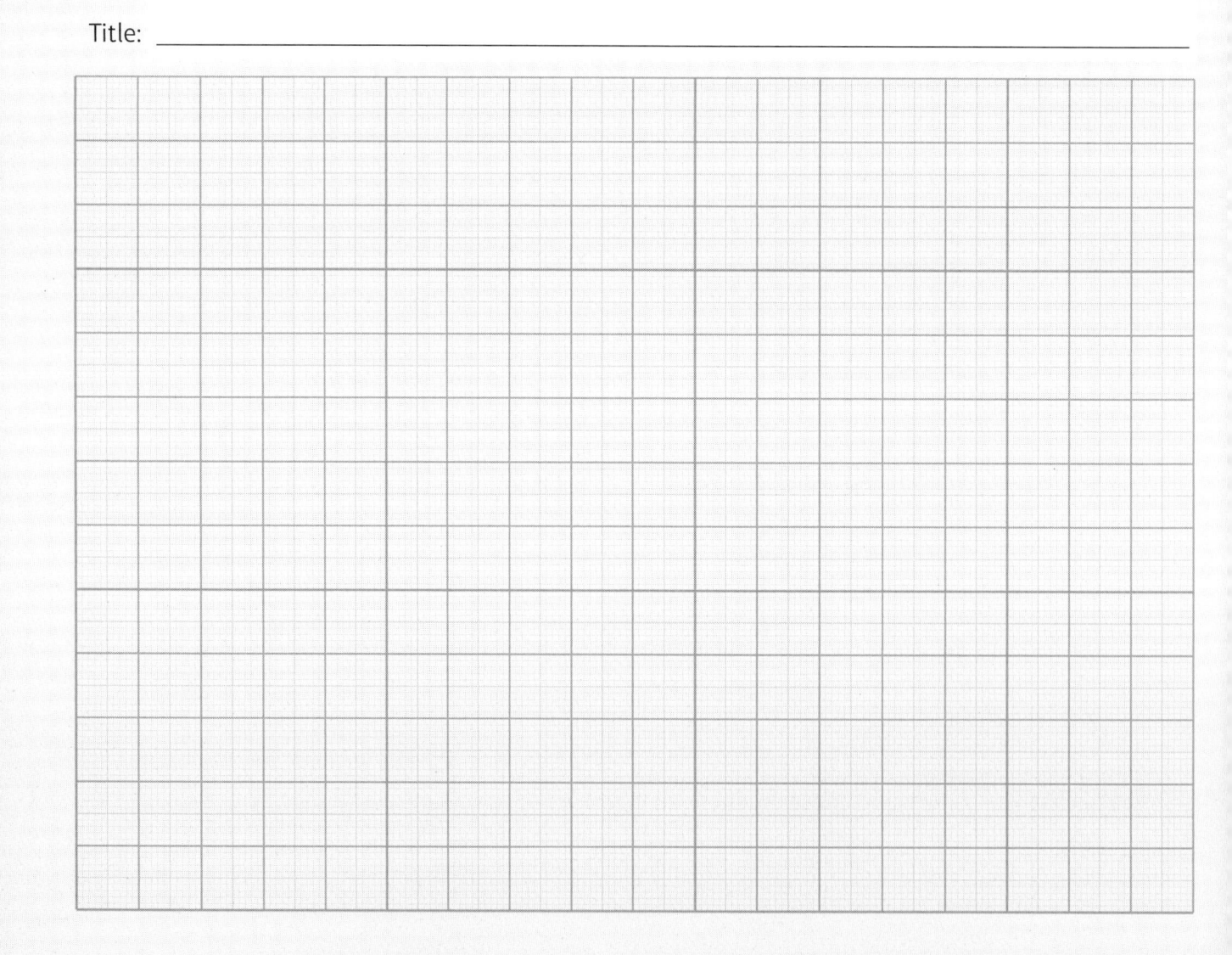

Title: _____

Chemistry 4: Energy and reactions

Checkpoint

Teacher comments

Look at the 'Skills you will develop' on page 46. In the boxes, indicate how confident you are at each skill.
What I will do to develop my skills more

Physics 1: Voltage, current and resistance

KS3 Science Lab Book

Getting started

Aims
- Describe how current flows in a parallel circuit.
- Calculate the resistance of a component.

Skills you will develop
- ☐ Consider the accuracy of measurements (voltage and current).
- ☐ Produce labelled drawings and diagrams (circuit diagrams).
- ☐ Draw reasoned conclusions from data.
- ☐ Use equations to perform calculations.

What you need to know before starting

✔ Draw circuit diagrams and the symbols for a lamp/bulb, a cell, a battery, a switch, a resistor, a voltmeter and an ammeter.
✔ Explain why a bulb lights when a circuit is completed.
✔ Identify series and parallel circuits.
✔ Measure current using an ammeter.
✔ Measure voltage using a voltmeter.

A cell's voltage is a measure of the force with which it can push current around a circuit. Other components in a circuit have **resistance**, which reduces the current. The greater the resistance of a component, the more it reduces the current.

There is a difference between the voltage on either side of a component. This voltage drop (or **potential difference**) is measured using a voltmeter.

Top Tip
*Find help on **circuit diagrams** in the Appendix (section S12).*

Starter questions

1

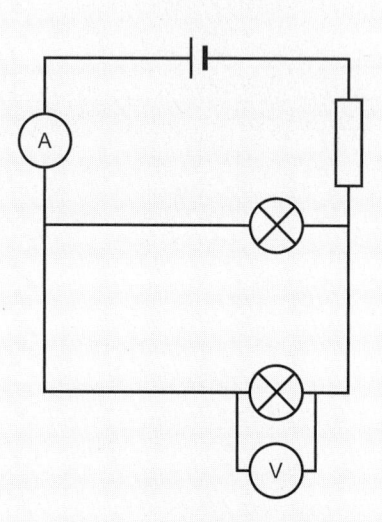

a On the circuit diagram, label each component with its name.

b Is this a parallel circuit or a series circuit? State how you know this.

_____

_____

Glossary: www.pearsonschools.co.uk/KS3LabGlossary

Physics 1: Voltage, current and resistance

KS3 Science Lab Book

2 Below each meter, record the reading shown. Remember to include the units.

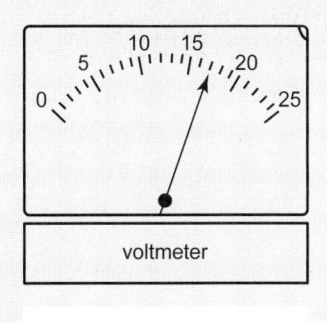

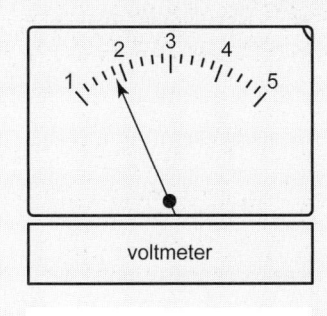

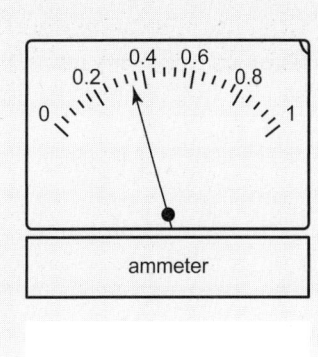

voltmeter	voltmeter	ammeter

Practical work

In this investigation you will first investigate how current flows in a parallel circuit. In the second part you will calculate resistance.

We can work out the resistance of a component if we know the current and the **potential difference** (voltage drop) across it. We use this **equation**:

$$\text{resistance (measured in ohms, } \Omega\text{)} = \frac{\text{potential difference (V)}}{\text{current (A)}}$$

Experiment 1 Current flow in parallel circuits

Apparatus	Safety ⚠
• cell (or battery or power pack) • connecting wires • ammeter • 3 bulbs	• If you are using a power pack, your teacher will tell you which voltage to use. Do not exceed this voltage.

Aim

1 Read the method below and write an aim for the experiment.

_____

_____

Method

In a series circuit, the current is the same wherever you measure it. It does not matter where you put the ammeter. What happens in a parallel circuit?
Build these circuits and record the ammeter readings in the table.

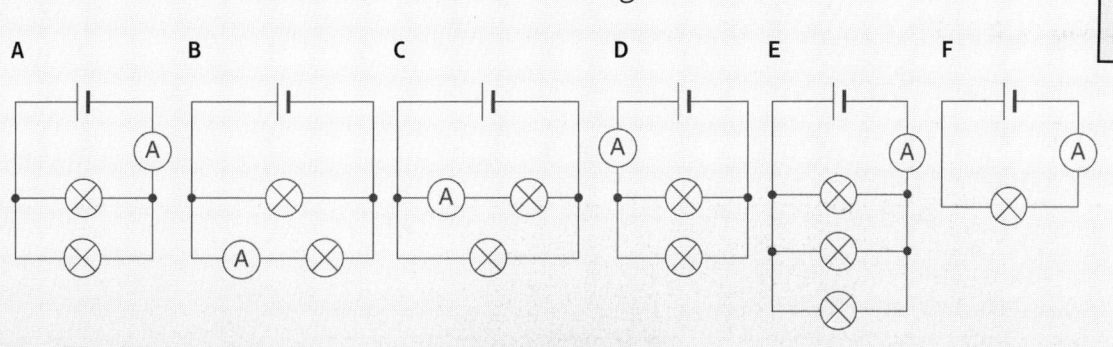

A   B   C   D   E   F

Top Tip

Find help on building circuits in the Appendix (section S12).

Glossary: www.pearsonschools.co.uk/KS3LabGlossary

Physics 1: Voltage, current and resistance

KS3 Science Lab Book

Recording your results

2   Record your readings in this table. You will need to add more headings.

Circuit		Circuit		Circuit	
A					
B					
		C			
		D			
				E	
				F	

Considering your results / Conclusions

3   Look at your results for circuits **A** to **D**.

   a   What do you notice about the currents in circuits **A** and **D**? _____

   _____

   b   What do you notice about the currents in circuits **B** and **C**? _____

   _____

   c   If you add the currents in circuits **B** and **C** together, what do you notice?

   _____

   _____

   d   Write a rule for what happens to the current as it flows around a parallel circuit.

   _____

   _____

   _____

4   Look at your results for circuits **E** and **F**. Write a rule for what happens to the current in the main part of a circuit when more bulbs are added in parallel.

   _____

   _____

Glossary: www.pearsonschools.co.uk/KS3LabGlossary

Physics 1: Voltage, current and resistance

KS3 Science Lab Book

Experiment 2 Calculating resistance

Apparatus
- cell (or battery or power pack)
- connecting wires
- ammeter
- voltmeter
- 2 resistors

Safety
- If you are using a power pack, your teacher will tell you which voltage to use. Do not exceed this voltage.

Aim
1 Read the method below and write an aim for the experiment.

Method
A Build the circuit on the right using resistor 1.

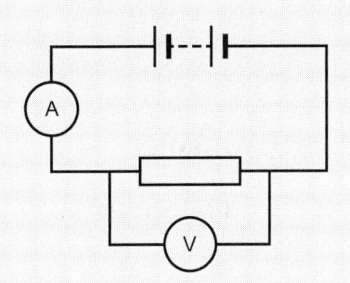

Top Tip
Find help on building circuits in the Appendix (section S12).

B Record the voltmeter and ammeter readings in the table below.
C Repeat steps **A** and **B** using the other resistor.

Recording your results
2 Record your readings in this table. You will need to add headings.

Component			
resistor 1			
resistor 2			

Considering your results / Conclusions
3 Complete the equations to calculate the resistance of resistor 1.

$$\text{resistance } (\Omega) = \frac{\text{potential difference (V)}}{\text{current (A)}}$$

$$\text{resistance} = \frac{_____ \text{ V}}{_____ \text{ A}}$$

resistance = _____ Ω

Glossary: www.pearsonschools.co.uk/KS3LabGlossary

Physics 1: Voltage, current and resistance

KS3 Science Lab Book

4 Calculate the resistance of resistor 2. Show your working.

resistance = _____

5 Explain which component would cause the greater reduction of current in a series circuit.

_____

_____

Check your understanding

1a Fill in the missing ammeter readings in these circuits.

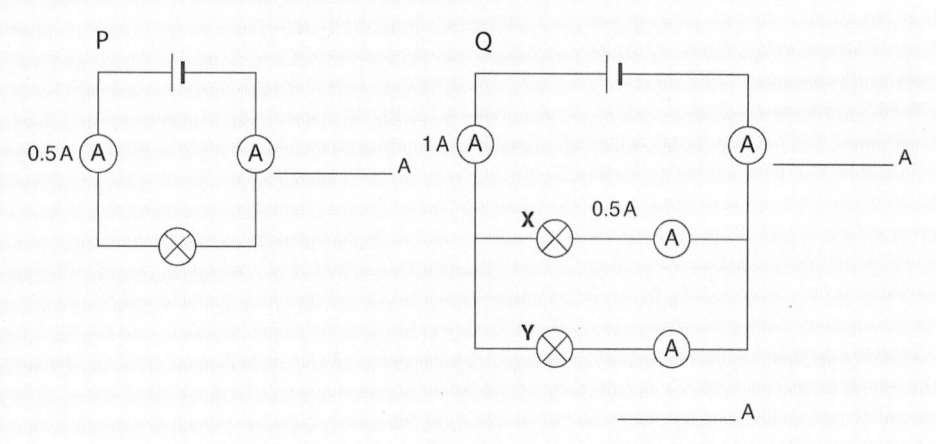

b In circuit P, add a component to measure the voltage drop across the lamp.

c A resistor is added in series to circuit **P**. What happens to the current? Tick *one* box.

☐ It will increase because there are more components for current to flow through.

☐ It will decrease because there is more resistance in the circuit.

☐ It will stay the same because resistors do not affect current.

☐ It will remain at 0 A because current does not flow through series circuits.

d In circuit **Q**, X and Y are similar bulbs. How do their brightnesses compare with one another?

_____

_____

Glossary: www.pearsonschools.co.uk/KS3LabGlossary

Physics 1: Voltage, current and resistance

e A third bulb is added in parallel to circuit **Q**. What happens to the current flowing through the cell? Tick *one* box.

☐ It will increase because there are more pathways for current to flow through.

☐ It will decrease because there are more pathways for current to flow through.

☐ It will stay the same because the bulbs will be equally bright.

☐ It will remain at 0 A because current does not flow through cells.

a Fill in the missing units in the table headings.

b Calculate the resistance of each resistor in the table.

Resistor	Voltage drop (_____)	Current (_____)	Resistance (_____)
A	12	2	
B	50	10	
C	20	4	
D	6	2	

Checkpoint

Teacher comments

Look at the 'Skills you will develop' on page 54. In the boxes, indicate how confident you are at each skill.

What I will do to develop my skills more

Physics 2: Investigating insulation

KS3 Science Lab Book

Getting started

Aim
- Find out whether the thickness of insulation affects energy transfer.

Skills you will develop
- ☐ Interpret and plot charts (**bar charts**).
- ☐ Evaluate investigations (including their accuracy).
- ☐ Use findings to develop further questions or ideas.

What you need to know before starting

✔ Describe how energy can be transferred by conduction, radiation and convection.
✔ Describe how energy is conducted better through some materials than others.
✔ Describe substances in terms of the particle model of matter.
✔ Recall the meanings of the terms: conductor, fluid, gas, insulator, liquid, particle model, solid, state of matter.

Energy is transferred by heating in different ways.

When a liquid **evaporates**, the faster moving, higher energy particles escape first (to form a gas). The remaining particles store less energy and so the temperature of the liquid is lower.

Convection occurs in fluids (liquids and gases). When part of a fluid is heated, the particles spread out and the fluid becomes less dense. This makes it rise, carrying the energy upwards.

When particles in solids gain energy, they vibrate faster and further. These vibrations (and their energy) are passed to neighbouring particles. This is **conduction**, which also happens in liquids (but not very well).

Any warm object gives out (infrared) **radiation**, which transfers energy from the object.

Starter questions

1 These instruments are all used to measure mass. The **accuracy** is shown as the possible error in the reading, and the ± symbol means 'plus or minus'. For example, if balance **X** shows a mass of 50 g, the true mass could be between 40 g and 60 g.

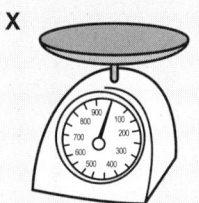

X
Range: 5 g to 5 kg
Accuracy: ± 10 g
Cost: £15

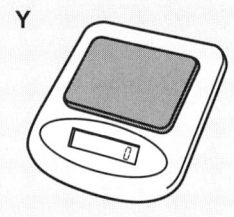

Y
Range: 0.1 g to 200 g
Accuracy: ± 0.1 g
Cost: £30

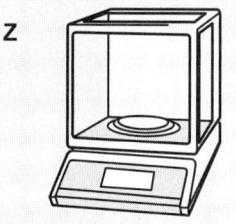

Z
Range: 0.2 mg to 65 g
Accuracy: ± 0.1 mg (0.0001 g)
Cost: £600

a Which instrument is the most accurate? _____

b Explain your answer to part **a**. _____

c Balance **Y** shows 104.0 g. State the lowest and highest values of the true mass.

Physics 2: Investigating insulation

KS3 Science Lab Book

d Explain which instrument is most suitable for measuring ingredients for a cake.

Practical work

Hot water inside a glass beaker transfers energy to the glass. This energy transfers from the inside surface of the beaker to its outside surface. It then transfers from the outside surface, and the beaker becomes cooler. You will test the **hypothesis** that the **speed** of cooling depends on the thickness of material around a beaker.

> **Top Tip**
> Find help on hypotheses in the Appendix (section S2).

Prediction

1 Explain whether you think thick or thin insulation will have more effect.

Apparatus

- 5 beakers
- 5 lids (for beakers)
- 5 thermometers
- fleece material
- hot water from the tap (not boiling water)
- rubber bands or sticky tape (to hold the fleece in place)
- stop clock

Safety

- Hot water can scald you.
- Take care when handling beakers of hot water.

Method

A Wrap fleece around five beakers. Use different numbers of layers.

B Pour hot water into each beaker and put the lids on.

C Write down the temperature of the water in each beaker. You will need to work in a team to read all the thermometers at the same time.

D After 5 minutes, record the temperatures again.

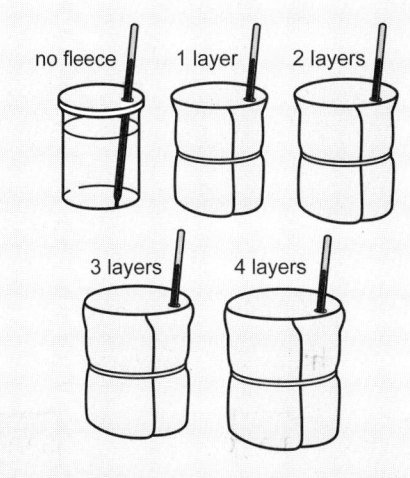

Physics 2: Investigating insulation

Recording your results

2 Complete this table. You will need to add one row for each beaker.

Number of layers	Temperature at start (°C)	Temperature at end (°C)	Temperature decrease (°C)
0	39	36	3
1	39	37	2
2	40	37	3
3	40	39	1°C

Top Tip
Find help on tables in the Appendix (section S13).

Considering your results / Conclusions

3a State the **independent variable**. _Number of layers_

b State the **dependent variable**. _tempreture decrease_

c List two **control variables**. _Time, type of beaker_

Top Tip
Find help on variables in the Appendix (section S6).

4 Draw a bar chart to show your results. Use the graph paper below.

Title: _____

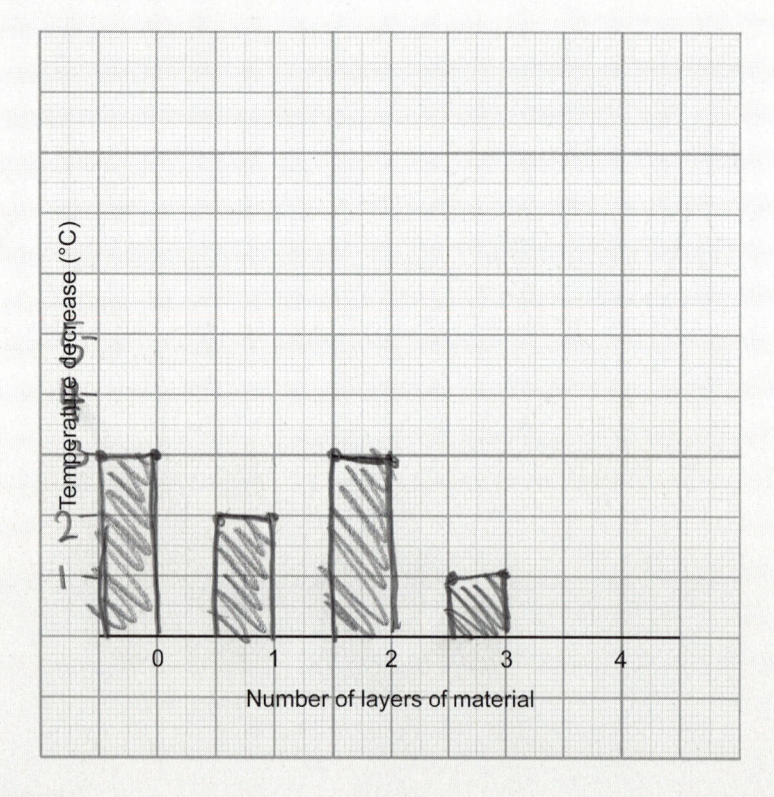

Top Tip
Find help on bar charts in the Appendix (section S16).

Physics 2: Investigating insulation

KS3 Science Lab Book

5a Which beaker had the smallest temperature change? _____

  b Describe how the number of layers of material affects the decrease in water temperature.
  _____
  _____

  c Use your scientific knowledge to explain your findings.
  _____
  _____
  _____
  _____

Evaluation

6a Name one variable that was not well controlled. _____

  b How could you control this variable better? _____
  _____
  _____

7a Do you think you have enough **evidence** to be sure of your answer to question **5b**? Explain your reasoning.
  _____
  _____
  _____
  _____

  b What could you do to check that your conclusion is correct? _____
  _____

8 Most lab thermometers measure to within 0.5 °C of the true temperature; others measure to 0.1 °C. Some temperature probes measure temperatures to two **decimal places**.

  a Which piece of apparatus is the most accurate?
  _____

  b Would using a temperature probe make your experiment better, and make you more certain of your conclusion? Explain your reasoning.
  _____
  _____
  _____

> **Top Tip**
>
> Find help on accuracy and decimal places in the Appendix (sections S10 and S22).

Glossary: www.pearsonschools.co.uk/KS3LabGlossary

Physics 2: Investigating insulation

Check your understanding

1. Some students took four beakers and covered three of them with different materials. They added hot water to all four beakers and put on cardboard lids. They measured the temperature of the water in each beaker. After 10 minutes they measured the temperatures again. Here are the results.

   For the uncovered beaker the temperature went down to 63 °C from 84 °C.
   Artificial fur: started at 82 °C. Ended at 74 °C.
   The paper had a drop of 15 °C (from the start temperature of 78 °C).
   Bubble wrap started at 80 °C and ended at 70 °C.

   Draw a table to show the students' results (including the temperature drop for each material).

   b State the independent variable. _____

   c State the dependent variable. _____

   In the evaluation, a student has written:

   To improve this experiment I would use a more accurate thermometer, which could measure ± 0.1 °C. Then I could be certain of my conclusion.

   d Explain whether or not this will improve the investigation.

   _____
   _____
   _____
   _____

Physics 2: Investigating insulation

Checkpoint

Teacher comments

Look at the 'Skills you will develop' on page 60. In the boxes, indicate how confident you are at each skill.
What I will do to develop my skills more

Physics 3: Investigating speed

KS3 Science Lab Book

Getting started

Aim
- Find out how some variables affect the speed of a toy car.

Skills you will develop
- ☐ Plan experiments (range, interval, number of readings).
- ☐ Use equations to perform calculations.
- ☐ Interpret graphs (line graphs, distance–time graphs).
- ☐ Consider the precision of measurements.
- ☐ Consider the accuracy of measurements.
- ☐ Identify and suggest reasons for anomalous measurements.

What you need to know before starting

✔ Recall some common units for measuring time, distance and speed.

✔ Use mathematical **equations** to perform calculations.

Speed is how far something travels in a certain time. This is the equation for calculating a speed:

$$\text{speed} = \frac{\text{distance}}{\text{time}} \quad \text{or} \quad S = \frac{D}{T}$$

Starter questions

1 A car travels 250 km in 5 hours. Calculate its speed. Show your working.

speed = _____

2 Precision is how close repeated readings are. More precise readings are more likely to be correct.

Three groups used different methods to measure a student's walking speed. The student's actual speed was 1.41 m/s.

	Walking speed (m/s)			
	1st try	**2nd try**	**3rd try**	**Mean**
Group A	1.50	1.42	1.31	
Group B	1.51	1.28	1.44	
Group C	1.41	1.43	1.39	

a Which group obtained the most precise results? _____

b Which of group B's readings was the most accurate? _____

Glossary: www.pearsonschools.co.uk/KS3LabGlossary

Physics 3: Investigating speed

c Calculate the **mean** speed from each group's results and complete the table.

d Explain why we calculate means of repeated readings in investigations.

_____
_____

> **Top Tip**
> Find help on means, precision and **accuracy** in the Appendix (sections S21 and S10).

Practical work

Many moving objects do not travel at a constant speed. The mean speed for a journey is the distance travelled in the whole journey divided by the time taken for the whole journey. You will investigate how some **variables** affect mean speed.

> **Top Tip**
> Find help on means in the Appendix (section S21).

Planning

1a Read the method and then add the name of the missing item to the apparatus list.

b Here are some **independent variables**. Choose two to investigate. Tick *two* boxes.

- ☐ height of the top of the slope
- ☐ surface covering of the ramp
- ☐ type of car (or trolley)
- ☐ mass of car (or trolley)

c Look at the apparatus you have available. For your first independent variable, state:
- the lowest and highest values of your independent variable (their **range**)

  lowest value: _____   highest value: _____

- how far apart your independent variable values will be (their **interval**).

  interval: _____

> **Top Tip**
> Find help on intervals and ranges in the Appendix (section S7).

Apparatus	Safety ⚠
• metre ruler or tape measure • toy car or trolley • ramp • blocks • masses • something to catch cars or trolleys (e.g. a cushion) • _____	• Use the cushion to ensure the car cannot hit anyone or fall on your feet.

Method

A Measure the distance the front of the car will travel. Record this value.

B Place the toy car or trolley at the top of the ramp. Hold it in place.

C At the same time as you let go of the car, start timing.

D Stop timing when the front of the car passes the end of the ramp.

E Repeat the timings twice more.

F Repeat steps **B** to **E** for different values of your 1st independent variable.

G Repeat the experiment for your 2nd independent variable.

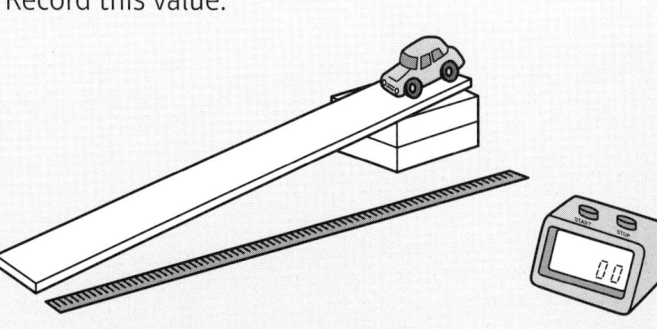

Physics 3: Investigating speed

KS3 Science Lab Book

Recording your results

2a Complete this table for the 1st independent variable. Add a heading to the first column.

_____	Time (s)			Mean time (s)	Distance (m)	Mean speed (m/s)
	1st try	2nd try	3rd try			

b Complete this table for the 2nd independent variable.

_____	Time (s)			Mean time (s)	Distance (m)	Mean speed (m/s)
	1st try	2nd try	3rd try			

Considering your results / Conclusions

3a Calculate the mean times. Add these times to the tables.

b Use the mean times to calculate the mean speeds. Add these to the tables.

4a Complete the sentences to describe the **correlations** you found.

1st independent variable: _____

Correlation: As the _____ increased, the mean speed _____.

2nd independent variable _____

Correlation: As the _____

increased, the mean speed _____.

> **Top Tip**
> Find help on means in the Appendix (section S21).

> **Top Tip**
> Find help on correlations in the Appendix (section S23).

Evaluation

5 You can be more certain that repeated readings are correct if they are precise.

a Which set of your time readings is the most precise? _____

b Explain your answer to part **a**. _____

> **Top Tip**
> Find help on precision and **anomalous** readings in the Appendix Appendix (sections S10 and S24).

Glossary: www.pearsonschools.co.uk/KS3LabGlossary

Physics 3: Investigating speed

c A reading that is far away from the others in a set is said to be anomalous. Do you have any anomalous readings? If so, state which ones they are.

d If you have any anomalous readings, suggest how they may have been caused.

6 Give a reason why calculating the mean of a set of repeated readings is useful.

> **Top Tip**
> Find help on means and accuracy in the Appendix (sections S21 and S10).

7 The diagram shows another version of this investigation, using light gates.

When the car enters the light gate, it cuts through a beam of light and starts a timer. When it leaves the light gate, the timer starts again.

Explain how using light gates would improve your experiment.

Physics 3: Investigating speed

Check your understanding

1 You can show how fast an object travelled during a journey using a type of **line graph** called a **distance–time graph**. A steeper line on the graph shows where the object was moving more quickly. A shallow line shows the object was moving more slowly. If the line is horizontal, the object was not moving.

Distance–time graph for a toy car

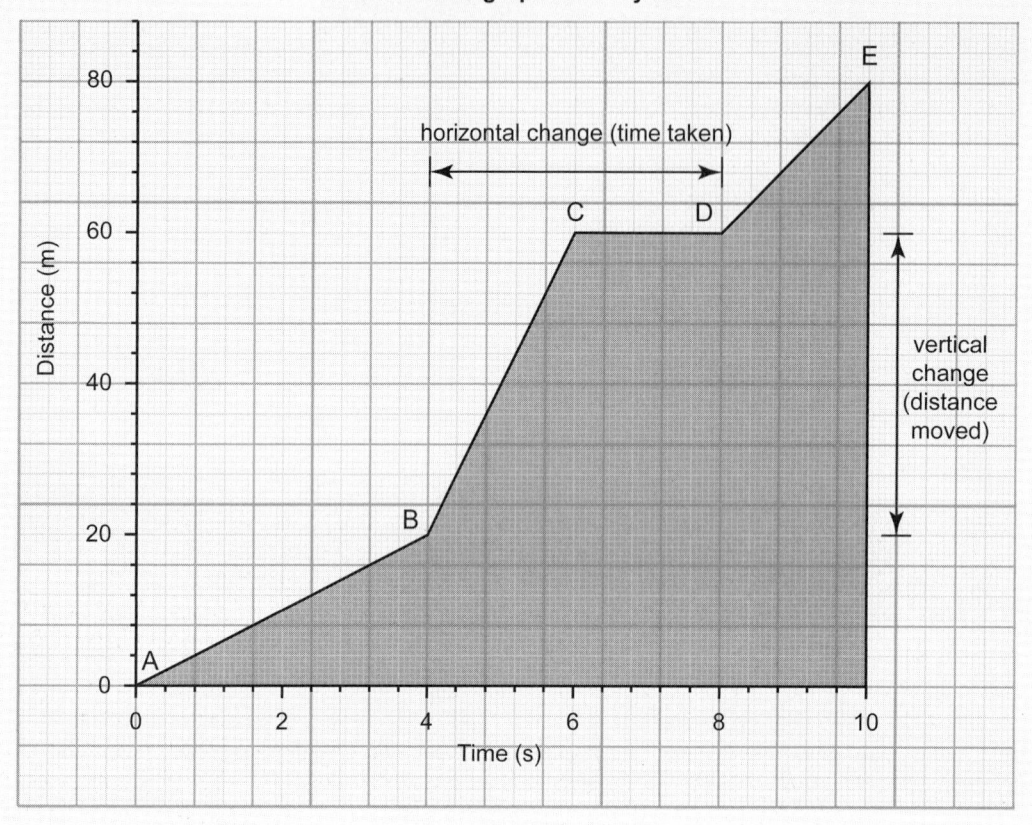

a Between which two points was the car moving fastest? _____

b Between which two points was the car stationary? _____

c Between which two points was the car moving, but at its slowest speed? _____

d You can calculate a speed from a distance–time graph by finding the gradient of the line. Work out the speed of the car between points B and C. The labels on the graph will help you. Show your working.

> **Top Tip**
> Find help on line graphs and gradients in the Appendix (section S17).

Speed = _____

Physics 3: Investigating speed

KS3 Science Lab Book

2 Some students used stop clocks to investigate how the height of a ramp affected the speed of a trolley rolling down it. They tried each height three times.

Height of ramp (cm)	1st try speed (cm/s)	2nd try speed (cm/s)	3rd try speed (cm/s)
2	16	20	18
4	30	31	31
6	42	44	37
8	51	2	58

a What was the range of the independent variable? _____

b What was the interval of the independent variable? _____

c For which height were their readings the most precise? _____

d For which height is one of their readings anomalous? _____

e Suggest how this anomalous reading was caused. _____

_____

3 Complete the table below.

Time taken (s)	Distance (m)	Speed (m/s)
0.5	14	
2		30
	90	45

> **Top Tip**
> Find help on changing the subject of an equation in the Appendix (section S19).

Checkpoint

Teacher comments

Look at the 'Skills you will develop' on page 66. In the boxes, indicate how confident you are at each skill.

What I will do to develop my skills more

Physics 4: Investigating electromagnets

KS3 Science Lab Book

Getting started

Aim	Skills you will develop
• Investigate the variables that affect the strength of an electromagnet.	☐ Plan experiments (range, interval). ☐ Identify independent, dependent and control variables. ☐ Describe how scientists publish their work.

What you need to know before starting

✔ Describe what an electromagnet is.

✔ Measure current using an ammeter.

✔ Recall how changes in voltage in a circuit affect the current.

In 1820, Danish scientist Hans Christian Ørsted discovered that current in a wire caused a **magnetic field**. His discovery was published as a paper in a **journal** (a scientific magazine). This helped William Sturgeon to make the first electromagnet in 1825.

Sturgeon also published his results in a paper and set up a new journal called the *Annals of Electricity, Magnetism and Chemistry*. This journal was peer-reviewed, which means that all the papers were inspected by other scientists to make sure that the experiments were well designed. Today, you can still be more certain of the findings published in a peer-reviewed journal.

Starter question

1. Scientists often investigate how changing an **independent variable** causes changes to a **dependent variable**. Imagine you are peer-reviewing an investigation report. Describe one thing you will check about the investigation.

   _____

   _____

   _____

> **Top Tip**
> Find help on **variables** and **peer review** in the Appendix (sections S6 and S3).

Practical work

You will investigate how the strength of an electromagnet is affected by the number of coils of wire, the current flowing and the core.

Planning

1. Complete the labels on the diagram on the following page.
2. Read Methods 1 and 2 and then complete the apparatus list.
3. Complete the safety box to describe one way of reducing the **risk** from this **hazard**.
4. In **Method 1**, you will change the number of coils.
   a. What will be the lowest and highest numbers of coils you will try (your **range**)?

   lowest: _____   highest: _____

> **Top Tip**
> Find help on hazards and risks in the Appendix (section S4).

Glossary: www.pearsonschools.co.uk/KS3LabGlossary

Physics 4: Investigating electromagnets

KS3 Science Lab Book

b What **interval** will you use (when changing the number of coils)?

interval: _____

5 In **Method 2**, you will change the voltage (which will change the current).

a What will be the lowest and highest voltages you will try?

lowest: _____   highest: _____

b What interval will you use between one voltage setting and the next?

interval: _____

6 Write a plan for Method 3 in the space provided on page 75.

> **Top Tip**
>
> Find help on intervals and ranges in the Appendix (section S7).

Apparatus
- insulated wire
- connecting wires
- low voltage DC **power** pack
- 2 crocodile clips
- paper clips
- iron rod or nail
- glass rod
- wooden rod or pencil
- _____

Safety ⚠
- The wire will get hot. Make sure you switch off the power pack between tests.
- _____
- _____
- _____

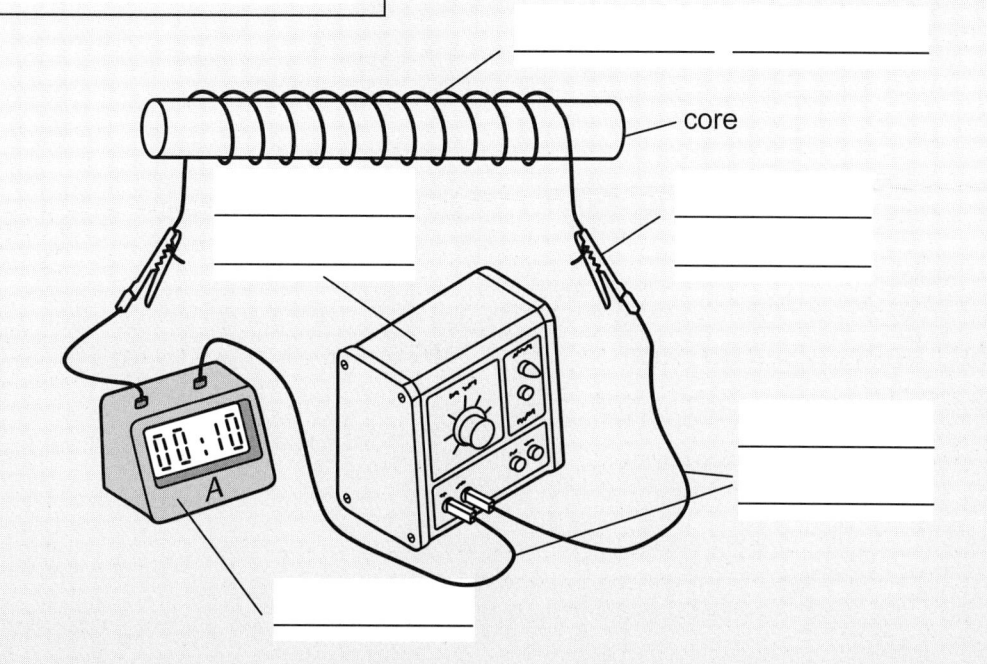

Method 1 Changing the number of coils of wire

A Make an electromagnet with 10 coils and an iron core.

B Switch on the electricity for a few seconds and see how many paper clips one end of the electromagnet picks up. Switch off again and record your result.

C Repeat steps **A** and **B** for different numbers of coils of wire. Keep the same setting on the power pack each time.

Glossary: www.pearsonschools.co.uk/KS3LabGlossary

Physics 4: Investigating electromagnets

KS3 Science Lab Book

Recording your results

7a Complete this table for your 1st independent variable (number of coils).

Number of coils	Number of paper clips picked up

Considering your results / Conclusions

8 What were your **control variables** in this experiment?

_____

_____

9 Complete this conclusion using one word from each set of brackets.

When there were more coils of wire, the electromagnet picked up _____ (more/fewer) paper clips. The more coils of wire, the _____ (stronger/weaker) the electromagnet.

Method 2 Changing the current

A Make an electromagnet with 20 coils of wire and an iron core.

B Set the voltage to 1 V and switch on the power pack. Read the ammeter and record the current. Switch off the power pack.

C Switch on the electricity for a few seconds and see how many paper clips you can pick up with one end of the electromagnet. Switch off the electricity and record your result.

D Repeat steps **B** and **C** for other voltages.

Recording your results

10 Complete this table for your 2nd independent variable (current).

Voltage (V)	Current (A)	Number of paper clips picked up

Considering your results / Conclusions

11 What were your control variables in this experiment?

_____

_____

Physics 4: Investigating electromagnets

KS3 Science Lab Book

12 Write a conclusion for how the current affects the electromagnet.

Method 3 Changing the core material

13 Write your plan below. Letter the steps.

Recording your results

14 Construct a table to record your results.

Considering your results / Conclusions

15 What were your control variables in this experiment?

16 Write a conclusion for how the core material affects the electromagnet.

Physics 4: Investigating electromagnets

KS3 Science Lab Book

Evaluation

17 Another way to measure the strength of the electromagnet is to use it to attract a piece of iron attached to a digital force meter. You can measure the force needed to separate the electromagnet from the piece of iron. Explain why this gives more accurate results.

> **Top Tip**
> Find help on **accuracy** and errors in the Appendix (section S10).

Check your understanding

1 Each part of this question describes a change that can be made to an electromagnet. What effect will each change have? Tick the correct boxes.

Change to electromagnet	Effect on electromagnet	
	Stronger magnetic field	**Weaker magnetic field**
a current through the wire is made smaller	☐	☐
b number of wire coils around the core is increased	☐	☐
c current through the wire is increased	☐	☐

2 *Nature* is a peer-reviewed journal. Explain what peer-reviewed means.

Checkpoint

Teacher comments

Look at the 'Skills you will develop' on page 72. In the boxes, indicate how confident you are at each skill.

What I will do to develop my skills more

Glossary: www.pearsonschools.co.uk/KS3LabGlossary

Skills appendix

KS3 Science Lab Book

S1 Models (Core Skill 1)

A **model** is a way of representing something difficult, complicated or invisible. It helps us to understand something more easily. Models are used to describe and explain how things work and to make **predictions**. Models are always simpler than what they are describing or explaining. This means that they may not be able to describe or explain all of an idea.

Physical models

Physical models are models that you can touch.

- Molecules are represented by spheres joined with sticks, to describe their shapes.
- A coiled spring toy can be used to represent wave motion.

Abstract models

Abstract models exist in our imagination, inside computers or as written symbols.

- Electrical current can be modelled by thinking about water flowing through pipes.
- In the particle theory, we imagine that everything is made up of particles that behave like tiny spheres, whizzing around and bouncing off one another.
- Mathematical **equations** are also abstract models (e.g. **speed** = distance/time).
- Computers use complex maths to model complicated systems (such as weather).
- Chemical equations model what happens during **chemical reactions**. For example:

    methane + oxygen → carbon dioxide + water

    $CH_4 + 2O_2 \rightarrow CO_2 + 2H_2O$

- Food chains and food webs are also abstract models.

S2 The scientific method (Core Skill 2 (and 15))

Scientific discoveries often start with observations that lead to scientific questions being asked about how or why something happens. A scientific question is one that can be answered by doing experiments or making further observations.

Scientists use a series of steps (called the scientific method) to answer their questions.

First, you think of an idea to explain something. This idea is a **hypothesis**.

You then test your hypothesis by doing an investigation. A **prediction** is what you think will happen in an investigation if the hypothesis is correct.

Investigations produce **data**. If your data matches your prediction, then the data provides **evidence** that your hypothesis is correct. We say that the evidence supports the hypothesis. If not, the evidence does not support the hypothesis.

If a hypothesis seems to be correct, then it can be tested again by using it to write more predictions. If the data from many investigations all support a hypothesis, the hypothesis becomes a **theory**. A theory is a hypothesis that has been well tested.

Scientists continue to test theories time and time again. As our knowledge of science changes over time, so do hypotheses and theories. You can never prove that a theory is true. Even the theories of really famous scientists have been replaced by new ideas.

> **Top Tips**
> - Think about using 'depends on' when you invent a hypothesis. You can often write a hypothesis in terms of 'the **dependent variable** depends on the **independent variable**'.
> - Think about using 'If ..., then ...' when you make a prediction. You can often write a prediction in terms of 'If I change the independent variable in a certain way, then the dependent variable will change in a certain way'.

Glossary: www.pearsonschools.co.uk/KS3LabGlossary

Skills appendix

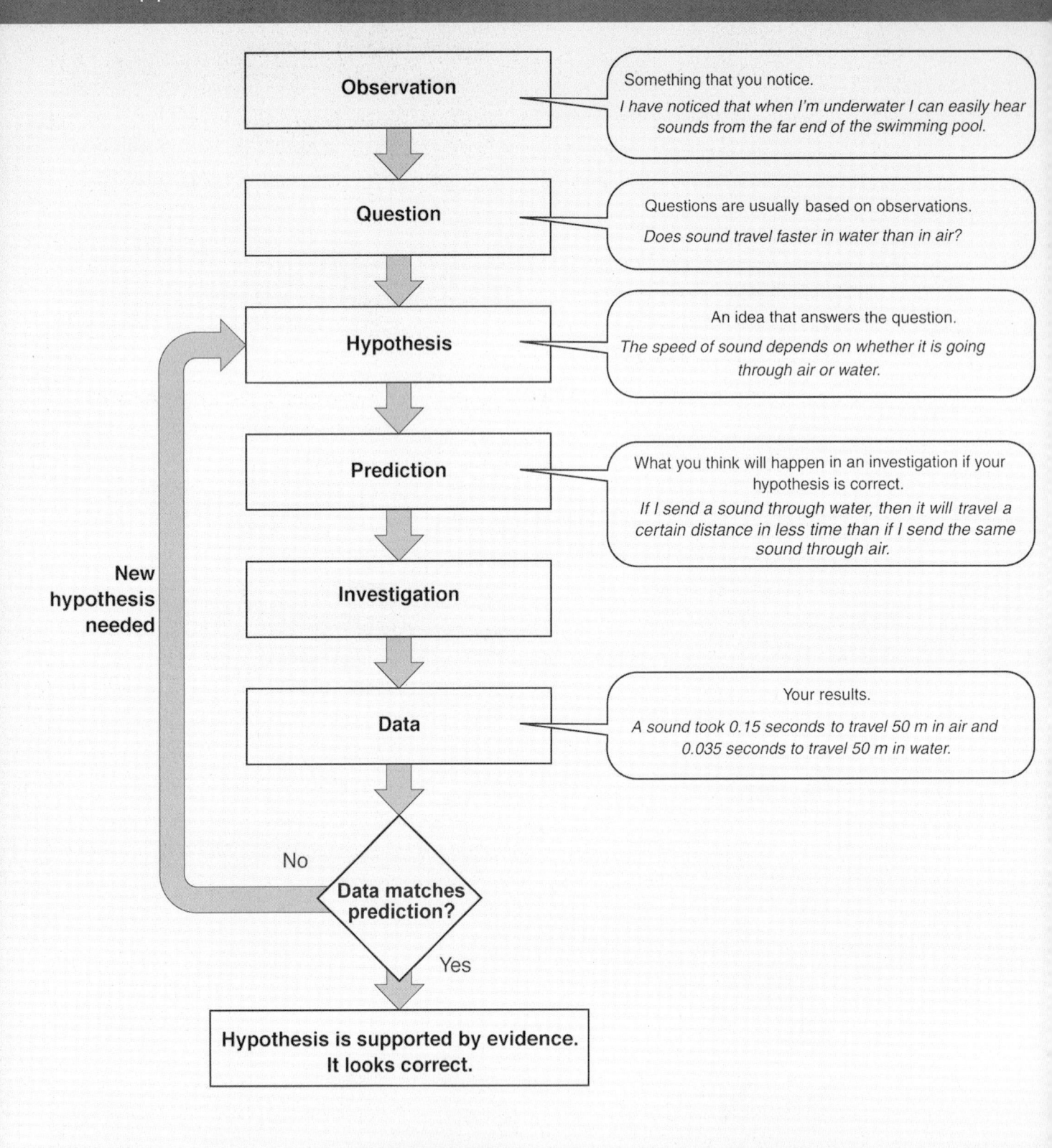

KS3 Science Lab Book

```
Observation ──→ Something that you notice.
                I have noticed that when I'm underwater I can easily hear
                sounds from the far end of the swimming pool.
     ↓
Question ──→ Questions are usually based on observations.
             Does sound travel faster in water than in air?
     ↓
Hypothesis ──→ An idea that answers the question.
               The speed of sound depends on whether it is going
               through air or water.
     ↓
Prediction ──→ What you think will happen in an investigation if your
               hypothesis is correct.
               If I send a sound through water, then it will travel a
               certain distance in less time than if I send the same
               sound through air.
     ↓
Investigation
     ↓
Data ──→ Your results.
         A sound took 0.15 seconds to travel 50 m in air and
         0.035 seconds to travel 50 m in water.
     ↓
Data matches prediction?
   No → New hypothesis needed (back to Hypothesis)
   Yes ↓
Hypothesis is supported by evidence.
It looks correct.
```

S3 Peer review (Core Skill 2)

Scientists tell others about their discoveries by publishing **papers** in **journals**.

Before a paper is published, it is often sent to other scientists working in the same area of science. These scientists evaluate the paper using criteria. They then say whether they think the paper should be published or not. This process is called **peer review**.

Some things that scientists look for when peer reviewing are:

- **control variables** have been identified and are properly controlled
- readings are accurate enough for a conclusion to be drawn
- readings are repeated and shown to be precise.

Glossary: www.pearsonschools.co.uk/KS3LabGlossary

Skills appendix

KS3 Science Lab Book

S4 Hazards and risks (Core Skill 3)

A **hazard** is something that may cause harm. A **risk** is the chance that a hazard will cause harm. When using hazardous substances, you must plan ways to reduce the risk that they will cause harm.

The diamond signs below are internationally agreed symbols found on the containers of some substances to warn of their hazards.

⚠	**Caution:** Should not cause serious harm but may cause skin or eye irritation, or make you choke if you breathe it in. Ways to reduce risks: Wear eye protection, wash off skin immediately with lots of water, avoid making powders go into the air. Wash your hands after use.

🧪	**Corrosive:** Attacks certain materials (such as metals, skin and stonework). Ways to reduce risks: Wear eye protection, wear skin protection.	🌳	**Dangerous to the environment:** May cause long-term damage to **habitats**. Ways to reduce risks: Use disposal methods that stop it getting into the environment.
🔥	**Flammable:** Catches fire easily. Ways to reduce risks: Keep away from naked flames, keep away from oxidising substances.	⭕	**Oxidising:** Provides oxygen (and makes things burn better). Ways to reduce risks: Keep away from naked flames, keep away from flammable substances.
☠	**Toxic:** Poisonous (may kill). Ways to reduce risks: Wear eye protection, wear skin protection, use in a fume cupboard.	💥	**Explosive:** May explode. Ways to reduce risks: Keep away from sources of heat, and flammable or oxidising substances.

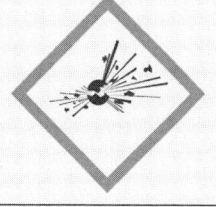

You may also see other hazard symbols, such as these ones.

⚠	This is a general warning symbol. It may be placed by some broken glass or a spilt chemical, or it may remind you to be careful when doing something or using certain equipment or substances.

⚡	This warns of a risk of getting an electric shock.	☣	This 'biohazard' symbol warns of organisms that may make you ill.

Some symbols tell you to do things to reduce the risk of a hazard causing harm.

👓	Wear eye protection.	🧼	Wash your hands.

Glossary: www.pearsonschools.co.uk/KS3LabGlossary

Skills appendix

S5 Samples (Core Skill 4)

A **sample** is a small part of a whole thing. We can use observations of a sample to say what the whole thing is like.

For example, a jar of seeds is 30 cm tall. If we count the seeds in the top 1 cm (a sample) we can **estimate** the number of seeds in the jar. (An estimate is an approximate value.)

×30 1 cm contains   35 seeds   ×30
     30 cm contains 1050 seeds

An advantage of using samples is that it takes less time to do an experiment. A disadvantage is that your findings may be inaccurate, unless you take a large enough sample.

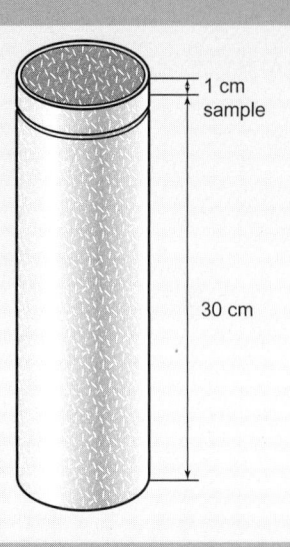

S6 Different types of variable (Core Skills 5, 6)

Anything that can change is called a **variable**.

A variable that you change in an investigation is the **independent variable**.

A variable that you measure in an investigation is a **dependent variable**.

Many experiments are designed to discover how changing an independent variable affects a dependent variable.

In an experiment, other variables may affect the dependent variable (not just the independent variable). These other variables must be controlled (stopped from changing). We call these **control variables**.

> **Top Tip**
>
> Remember which is which by thinking: 'I am **in** charge of the **in**dependent variable'.

> An athlete runs at different **speeds** on a treadmill. Her heartbeat rate is measured.
>
> The variable being changed is the speed of the treadmill. This is the independent variable. Its value does not depend on other variables.
>
> The variable being measured is the heartbeat rate. This is the dependent variable. Its value depends on other variables, such as the speed of the treadmill.

S7 Trial runs (Core Skills 5)

When you plan an investigation you often need to decide:
- the **independent variable** to change
- the **dependent variable** to measure
- the **range** of values for your independent variable. In science, the range is the difference between the highest and lowest values
- the **interval** (difference) between your independent variable values
- the number of measurements to make.

Skills appendix

KS3 Science Lab Book

A **trial run** (or 'preliminary task') is when you carry out your planned experiment with a limited number of values for the independent variable. It helps you to decide how best to carry out your full investigation. Your choices can affect the conclusion that you can draw.

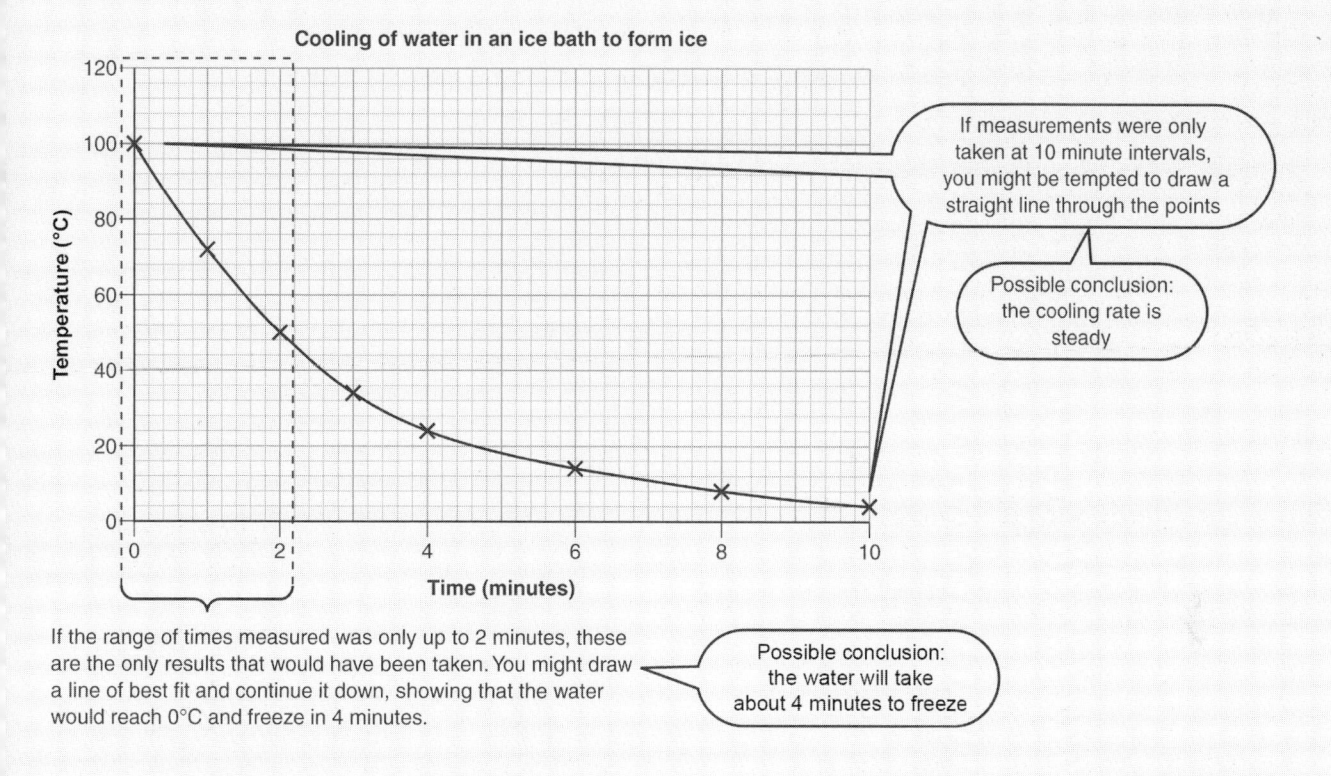

Cooling of water in an ice bath to form ice

If measurements were only taken at 10 minute intervals, you might be tempted to draw a straight line through the points

Possible conclusion: the cooling rate is steady

If the range of times measured was only up to 2 minutes, these are the only results that would have been taken. You might draw a line of best fit and continue it down, showing that the water would reach 0°C and freeze in 4 minutes.

Possible conclusion: the water will take about 4 minutes to freeze

In the example, the temperature of some water is being measured as it cools in an ice bath to find out how long it takes to freeze. A trial run would:

- find out what the range should be for the water to be frozen at the end. (Look at the graph. The water has still not frozen after 10 minutes.)
- find out what intervals to use to make sure that we can see the pattern of cooling. (Look at the graph. The pattern of cooling is a curve and not a straight line.)
- test that the method works as you planned and is safe.

S8 The Bunsen burner (Core Skills 8 (and 3))

- If your Bunsen burner goes out, turn off the gas at the gas tap straight away.
- Always let a Bunsen burner cool down before you put it away.
- Never take a Bunsen burner apart unless you are told to do so by your teacher.
- Wear eye protection.

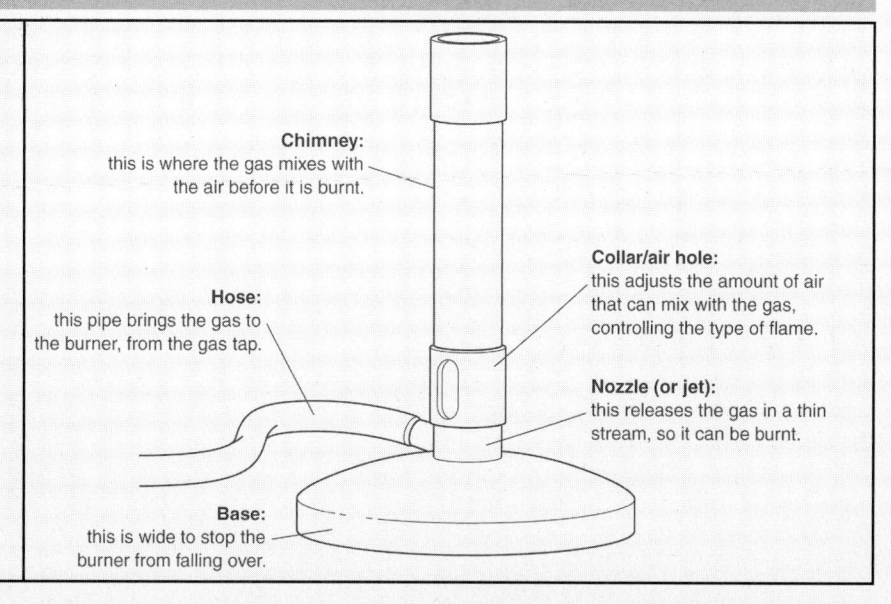

Chimney: this is where the gas mixes with the air before it is burnt.

Hose: this pipe brings the gas to the burner, from the gas tap.

Collar/air hole: this adjusts the amount of air that can mix with the gas, controlling the type of flame.

Nozzle (or jet): this releases the gas in a thin stream, so it can be burnt.

Base: this is wide to stop the burner from falling over.

Skills appendix

KS3 Science Lab Book

Every time you use a Bunsen burner, you should follow these steps:

A Check the hose for breaks and holes. If it is damaged, return the burner and tubing to your teacher.
B Connect the hose to the gas tap but do not turn it on yet.
C Check that the air hole in the collar of the Bunsen burner is closed.
D Hold a burning splint a little distance (about 2 cm) above the top of the chimney of the Bunsen burner.
E Turn on the gas at the gas tap.
F The Bunsen burner will now light and give you a yellow flame.
G Turn down the gas supply at the gas tap until you have the size of flame needed for your experiment.
H After using the burner, close the air hole (so the flame is yellow). Then turn off the gas at the gas tap.

The table below shows the different types of flame.

Type of flame	Safety	Medium	Roaring
Type of air hole	closed	half open	fully open
Amount of air mixing with gas	little	some	lots
Amount of noise	quiet	audible	noisy
Main colour of flame	yellow	blue	blue (the hottest part is just above the pale blue cone)
Use	safety (not used for heating)	heating gently (e.g. liquids in a tube)	heating strongly (e.g. a large beaker of water)

S9 Measuring volumes (Core Skill 10)

If you look carefully at the liquid in a tube, it goes up at the sides of the tube. The curved shape is the meniscus. Take your reading from the bottom of the meniscus.

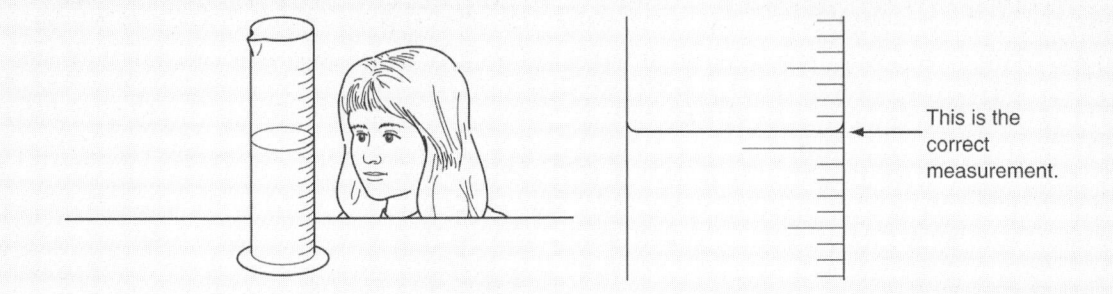

Some measuring cylinders are marked in cm^3 (centimetres cubed, cubic centimetres, sometimes written as cc), and some in ml (millilitres). 1 cm^3 is the same volume as 1 ml.

Glossary: www.pearsonschools.co.uk/KS3LabGlossary

Skills appendix

KS3 Science Lab Book

S10 Accuracy and precision (Core Skills 10, 11 (and 18, 19, 25))

Precision is how close repeated measurements are.

Accuracy is how close a measurement is to its true value. Accurate measurements may or may not be precise. Similarly, precise measurements may or may not be accurate.

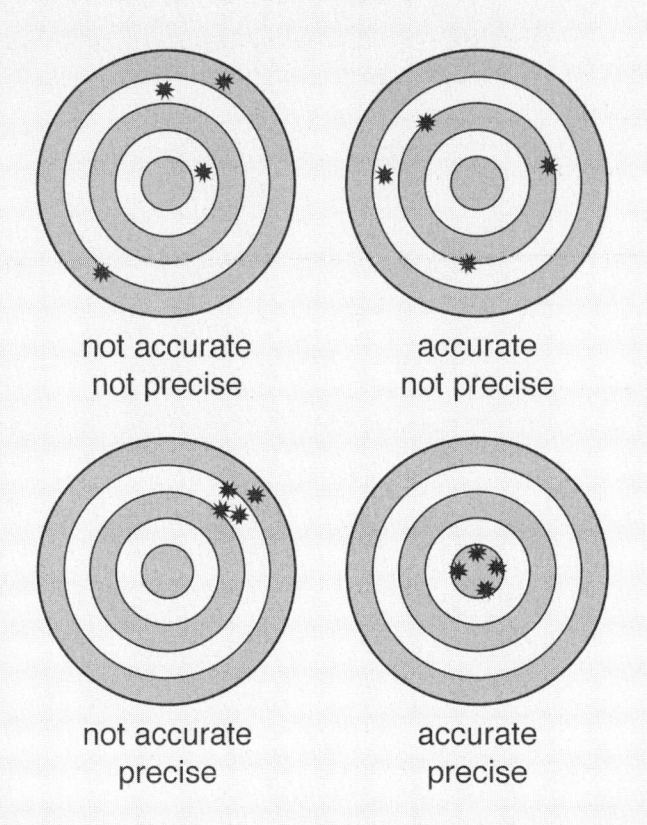

Top Tip

*It does not make sense to measure huge distances to the nearest millimetre, so you need to consider what is an appropriate level of accuracy. It might help to think about how many **significant figures** you need in your **data**.*

not accurate
not precise

accurate
not precise

not accurate
precise

accurate
precise

S11 Drawing apparatus (Core Skill 12)

Usually in science we draw diagrams of apparatus rather than pictures. Diagrams are easier to draw, and make it easier to see how the apparatus is joined together.

Imagine the apparatus cut in half. You draw what you would see from the side – this is called a cross-section diagram. Here are some standard diagrams that you should use.

Glossary: www.pearsonschools.co.uk/KS3LabGlossary

Skills appendix

Apparatus	Name	Diagram	What it is used for
	test tube		storing or mixing solids and liquids
	boiling tube		heating solids and liquids
	beaker		holding liquids or solids
	conical flask		holding and mixing liquids
	round-bottom flask		heating liquids
	measuring cylinder		measuring volumes of liquids
	Liebig condenser		cooling a vapour and condensing it into a liquid
	tripod		heating a beaker, flask or crucible over a Bunsen burner
	gauze	----------------	supporting a beaker or flask and spreading the heat from the flame
	Bunsen burner	HEAT	heating things
	evaporating basin		evaporating the water from a solution
	filter funnel (with paper)		separating an insoluble solid from a liquid
	rubber bung		keeping things in a tube or flask
	rubber bung with a hole		the hole is so that a tube or thermometer can be put into the liquid without any gases escaping

Scientific diagrams show how pieces of apparatus are put together to do practical work.

Glossary: www.pearsonschools.co.uk/KS3LabGlossary

Skills appendix

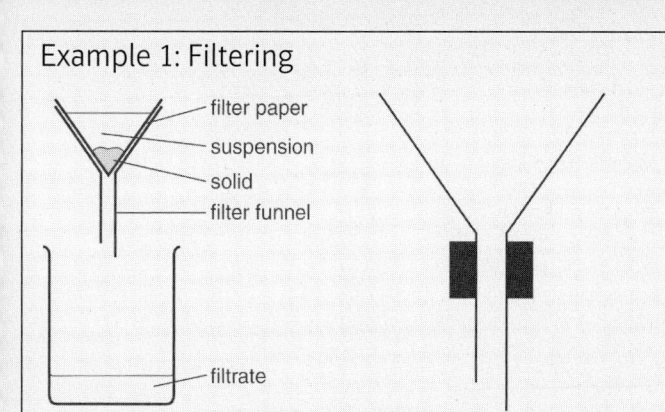

KS3 Science Lab Book

Example 1: Filtering

filter paper
suspension
solid
filter funnel
filtrate

You do not usually need to show the clamps and stands. Clamps can be shown like this.

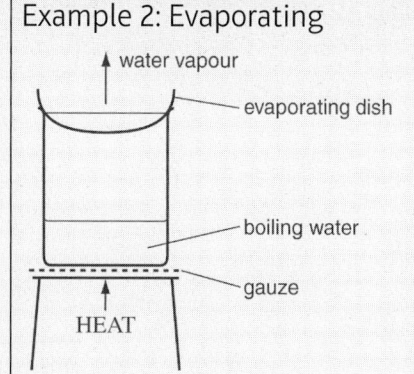

Example 2: Evaporating

water vapour
evaporating dish
boiling water
gauze
HEAT

You can use an arrow to show heat instead of drawing a Bunsen burner.

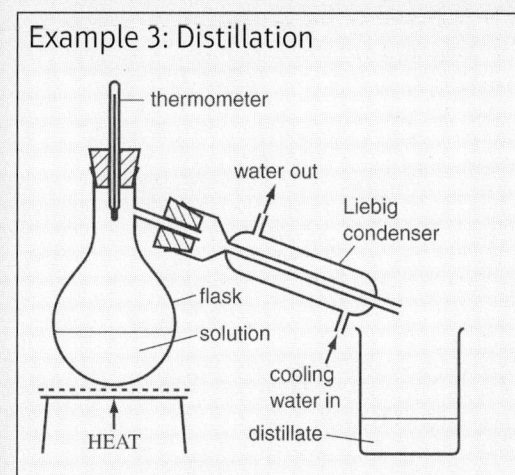

Example 3: Distillation

thermometer
water out
Liebig condenser
flask
solution
cooling water in
distillate
HEAT

This is a much more complicated diagram. Look carefully at the bungs. See how the diagram shows that the thermometer and tubes go through the middle of the bungs. Be careful that you don't 'block off' tubes that are really open. See how the 'water in' and 'water out' tubes are left open at the ends.

S12 Building circuits (Core Skill 12)

Building circuits is easier if you use **circuit diagrams**. Symbols represent the components.

cell (the + and − labels are optional)		ammeter (measures current in amps (A))	
battery (two or more cells connected together)		voltmeter (measures voltage or **potential difference** in volts (V))	
switch		resistor	
bulb (lamp)		motor	

First, collect all the components you need. You can work out how many wires you need by counting the number of pieces of wire between the components. This circuit needs four wires.

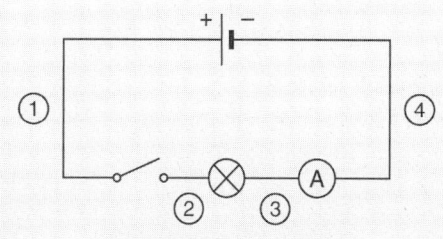

This circuit needs four wires

Glossary: www.pearsonschools.co.uk/KS3LabGlossary

85

Skills appendix

KS3 Science Lab Book

Follow the circuit diagram around and put in one component at a time, like this.

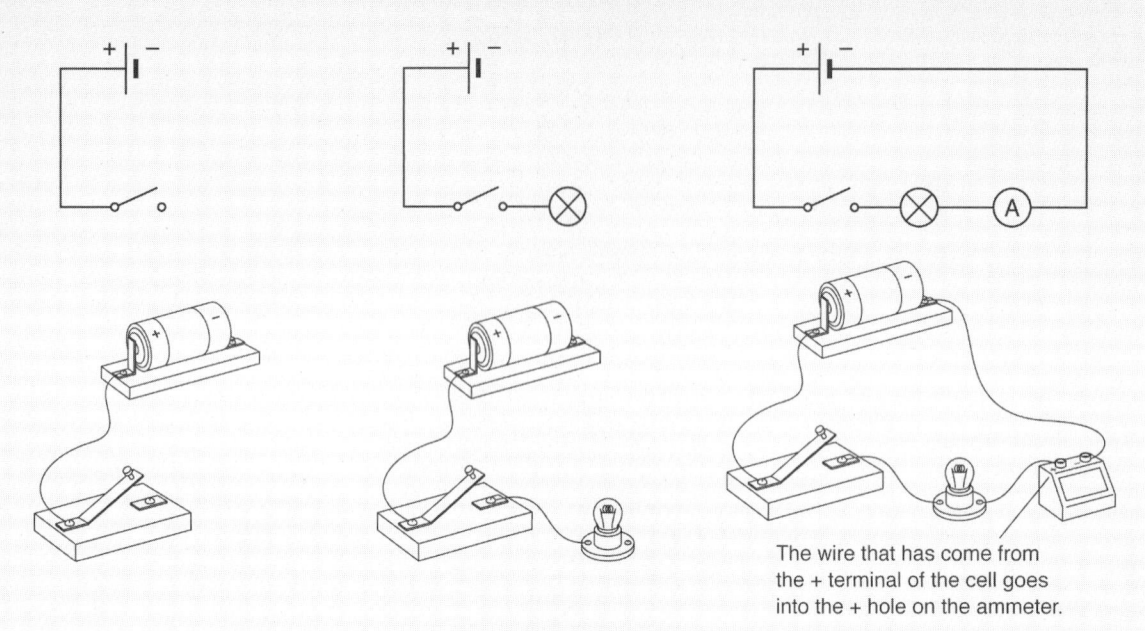

The wire that has come from the + terminal of the cell goes into the + hole on the ammeter.

Voltmeters in series circuits

When you are building a circuit with voltmeters, it is easier if you ignore the voltmeters to start with.

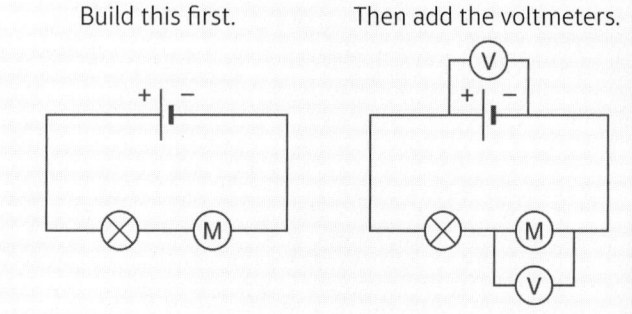

Build this first.   Then add the voltmeters.

Parallel circuits

Building parallel circuits is easy if you look at one branch of the circuit at a time.

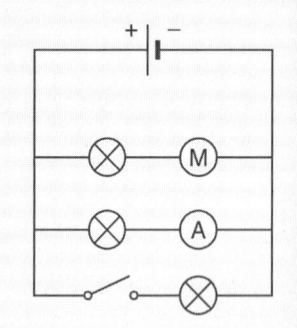

Instead of trying to build this circuit all in one go, take one piece at a time. First, build the top part, like this.

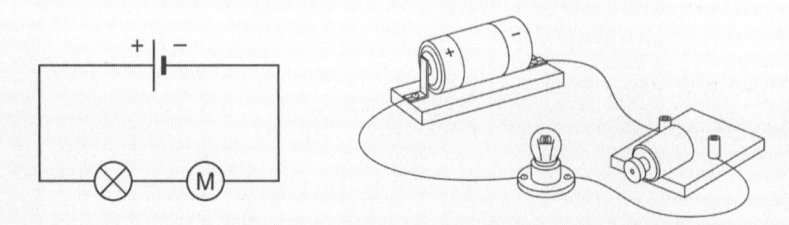

Glossary: www.pearsonschools.co.uk/KS3LabGlossary

Skills appendix

Then make the branches.

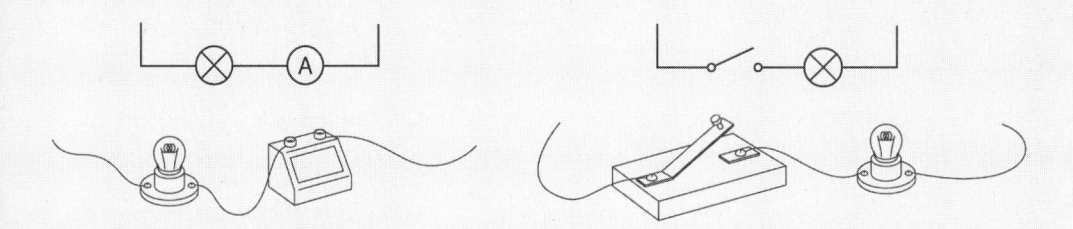

Then put them all together.

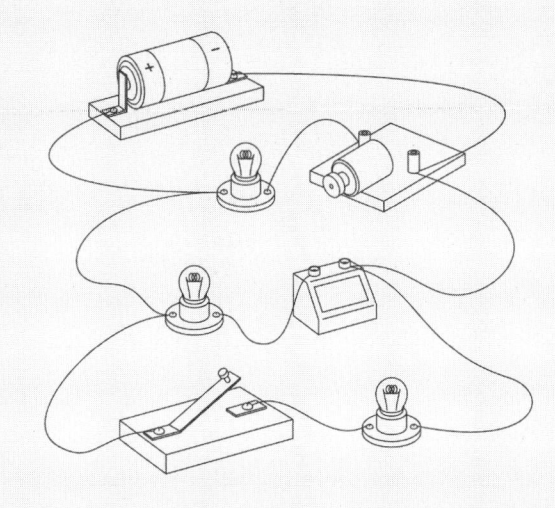

S13 Tables (Core Skill 13)

A table is a way of showing a lot of information in a way that is easy to read. Ordering the information in a table (e.g. numerical order, alphabetical order) makes it easier to see patterns or to identify certain values.

The table below shows the results of an experiment to discover how long it takes different amounts of sugar to dissolve in hot water. The call-outs explain how to construct a good results table.

The **independent variable** (what you change) always goes in the first column.

These are the amounts of sugar that will be tested.

Amount of sugar (spatulas)	Time to dissolve (minutes)
1	
2	
3	
4	
5	

The **dependent variable** (what you measure) goes in the other column.

Record the units. Separate them from the title using a stroke or brackets. For example, /minutes or (minutes).

Use a ruler.

If you investigate more than one independent variable, your table will need extra columns:

| Amount of sugar (spatulas) | Time to dissolve (minutes) ||
	Hot water	Cold water
1		
2		
3		
4		
5		

This heading applies to both of the columns beneath it.

Glossary: www.pearsonschools.co.uk/KS3LabGlossary

Skills appendix

KS3 Science Lab Book

S14 Chemical equations (Core Skill 14 (and 1))

Chemical reactions can be described using **models** called **equations**. These use words or chemical symbols. An equation shows the substances in a reaction. The substances at the start of a reaction (the **reactants**) are on the left of the equation. The substances that the reaction forms (the **products**) are on the right. The arrow shows the direction of the reaction and is drawn from the reactants to the products.

$$\underbrace{\text{copper oxide} + \text{sulfuric acid}}_{\text{reactants}} \rightarrow \underbrace{\text{copper sulfate} + \text{water}}_{\text{products}}$$

$$\underbrace{CuO + H_2SO_4}_{\text{reactants}} \rightarrow \underbrace{CuSO_4 + H_2O}_{\text{products}}$$

S15 Ways of presenting data (Core Skill 16)

When you have collected **data**, you display it in a way that makes it easy to identify differences, trends and patterns. The table describes some presentation methods.

Method of presentation	When used ...
tables	show items in a certain order (e.g. numerical order, alphabetical order). Tables help to identify patterns or the best and worst things in a list.
bar charts	show how things compare using lengths of bars
frequency diagrams	show the number of times something happens (the frequency)
line graphs	show how a **variable** changes over time
scatter graphs	show links (**relationships**) between two variables – how one variable changes when another variable changes
pie charts	show the proportions of a total contributed by different items (e.g. the proportions of students who get to school by bus, car, bike, on foot)
Venn diagrams	show how groups of items are the same or different
flow diagrams	show a sequence of information
labelled drawings and diagrams	simple pictures in which labels are used to name items and describe and explain processes

S16 Bar charts (Core Skill 16)

A **bar chart** shows how things compare, using lengths of bars.

There are gaps between the bars for an **independent variable** that is:

- in words, such as colours or foods (this is called **qualitative data**)

or

- in numbers that can only have certain values, such as shoe size (this is called **discrete data**).

The bar chart on the following page shows the **data** in this table.

Breakfast food	Number of people
cereal	15
toast	7
crisps or chocolate	2
nothing	6

Glossary: www.pearsonschools.co.uk/KS3LabGlossary

Skills appendix

KS3 Science Lab Book

Annotations on the bar chart:
- Choose a scale that lets you use as much of the graph paper as possible.
- Space numbers evenly.
- Dependent variable on the vertical (y) axis.
- Label the axes clearly using the table headings.
- A bar chart needs a title to describe what it shows.
- The bars can be displayed in any order. But you will see patterns more easily if they are shown in order of size.
- Use graph or squared paper.
- Use a ruler to draw straight lines.
- Independent variable on the horizontal (x) axis.

Bar chart: "What Class 7B had for breakfast" — Number of people vs Breakfast food: cereal 15, toast 7, nothing 6, crisps or chocolate 2.

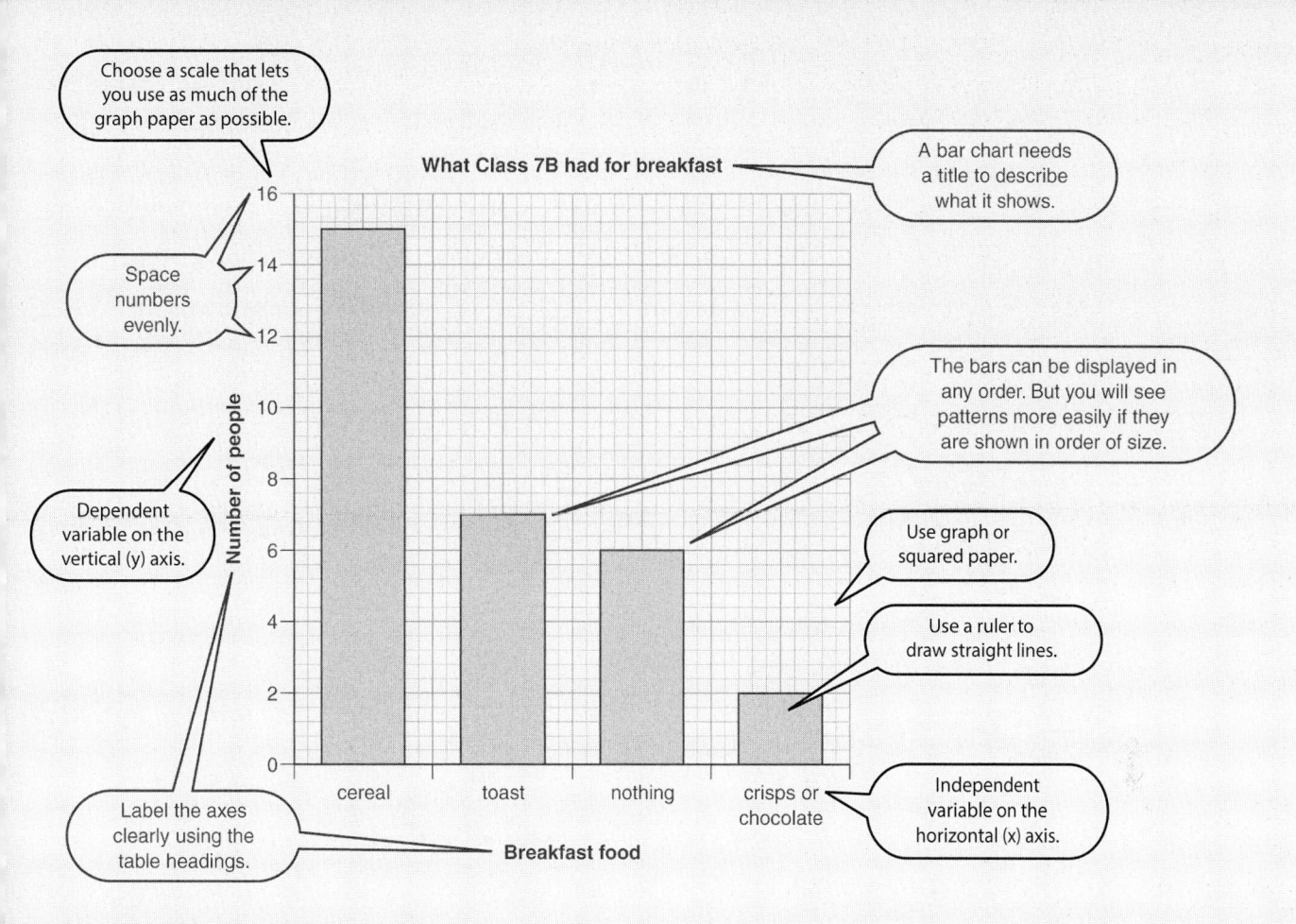

Working out the scale

You need to use scales that let your graph fill as much of the graph paper as possible.

A First, look at the table of results and work out the largest number for each axis.

B Count the squares on your graph paper. Can you make the number of squares match the largest number? If there are not enough then try again, counting in 2s, 5s, 10s, 100s and so on, until you find a scale that fits on the paper.

S17 Line graphs (Core Skill 16)

Line graphs show how one **variable** changes as another (usually time) changes.

You can use a line graph:
- when you know that the two variables are linked
- when both variables are quantitative (written as numbers).

We plot our **data** as points. We then join the points with straight lines. We can use the lines to **estimate** data values between our points.

> **Top Tip**
>
> *Scatter graphs are similar but are used to find a **relationship** between two variables (see S18).*

Glossary: www.pearsonschools.co.uk/KS3LabGlossary

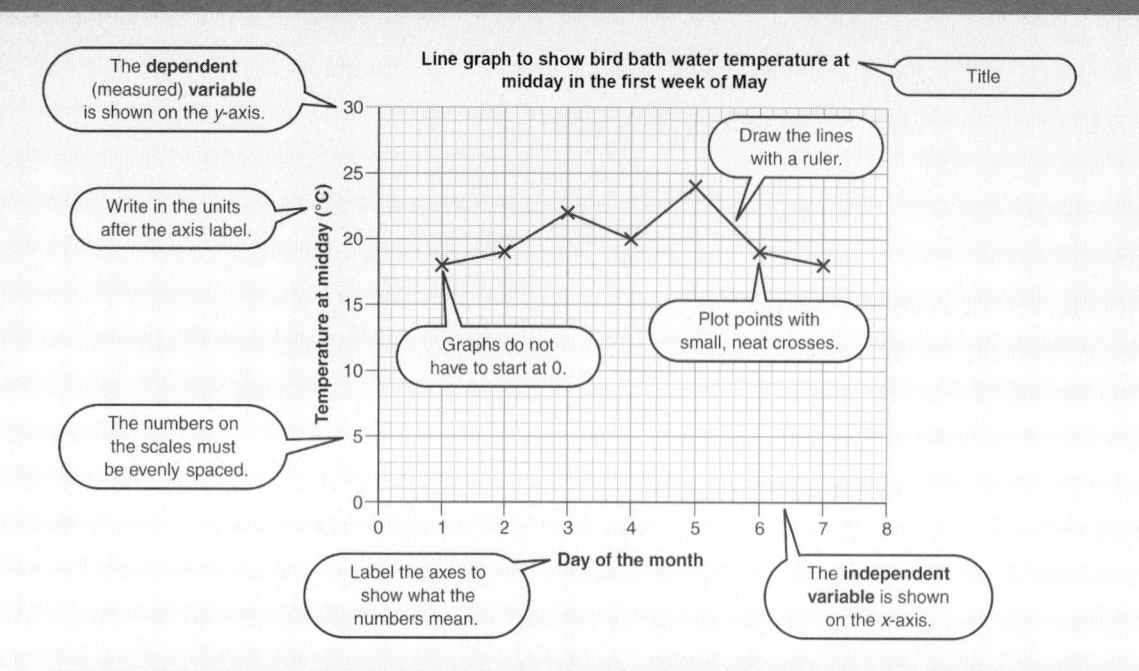

Skills appendix | KS3 Science Lab Book

Line graph to show bird bath water temperature at midday in the first week of May

Annotations:
- The **dependent** (measured) **variable** is shown on the *y*-axis.
- Write in the units after the axis label.
- The numbers on the scales must be evenly spaced.
- Title
- Draw the lines with a ruler.
- Plot points with small, neat crosses.
- Graphs do not have to start at 0.
- Label the axes to show what the numbers mean.
- The **independent variable** is shown on the *x*-axis.

y-axis: Temperature at midday (°C)
x-axis: Day of the month

Top Tip
Look at S16 for help on working out scales for axes.

S18 Scatter graphs (Core Skills 16, 20, 22)

We use **scatter graphs** are used to find out whether there is a link (**correlation** or **relationship**) between two **variables**. You can use a scatter graph when both variables are quantitative (written as numbers).

On the scatter graph below, the **independent variable** is the mass hung on a spring. The **dependent variable** is the **extension** (stretching) of the spring. The points form a roughly straight line, which shows that there is a correlation: the heavier the mass, the greater the extension.

Top Tip
Line graphs are similar but are used when you know there is a link between two variables. Line graphs are usually used to show how a variable changes with time (see S17).

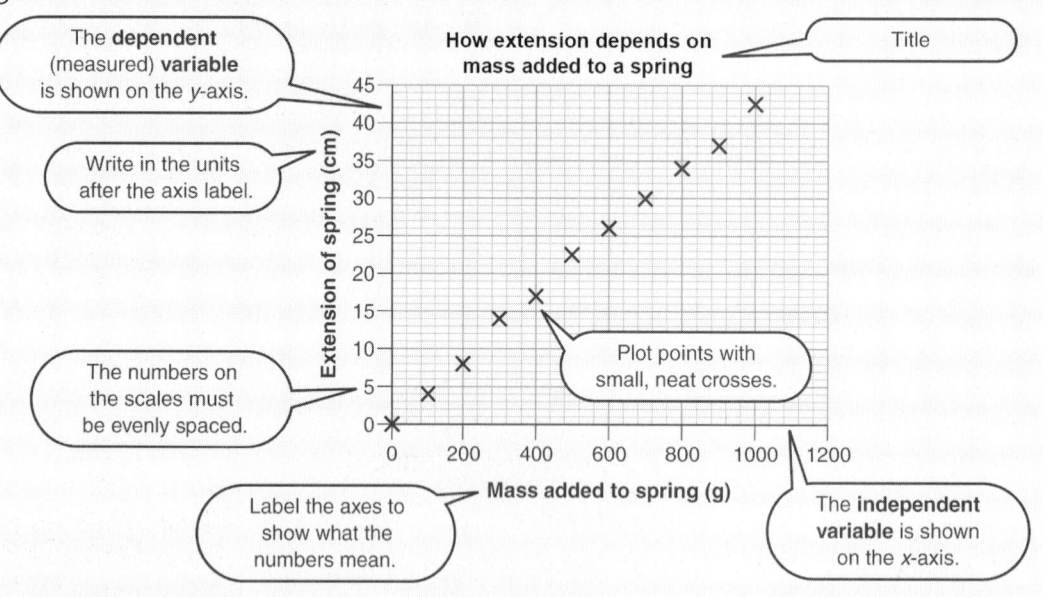

How extension depends on mass added to a spring

Annotations:
- The **dependent** (measured) **variable** is shown on the *y*-axis.
- Write in the units after the axis label.
- The numbers on the scales must be evenly spaced.
- Title
- Plot points with small, neat crosses.
- Label the axes to show what the numbers mean.
- The **independent variable** is shown on the *x*-axis.

y-axis: Extension of spring (cm)
x-axis: Mass added to spring (g)

Top Tip
Look at S16 for help on working out scales for axes.

Lines of best fit

The points on the scatter graph on the previous page follow a roughly straight line. There are some slightly inaccurate measurements, so the points do not line up exactly. However, we can still draw a line to show the correlation (relationship) between the two variables. This line is a **line of best fit** because it does not go exactly through all the points.

Glossary: www.pearsonschools.co.uk/KS3LabGlossary

Skills appendix

A line of best fit goes through the middle of your points, so that about half the points are above the line and half are below it.

A line of best fit does not need to go through the origin.

We can use the line to **estimate** values between the plotted points. We can also extend the line to estimate values beyond the **range** of measurements in an experiment.

Ignore **anomalous** results when drawing a **line of best fit**.

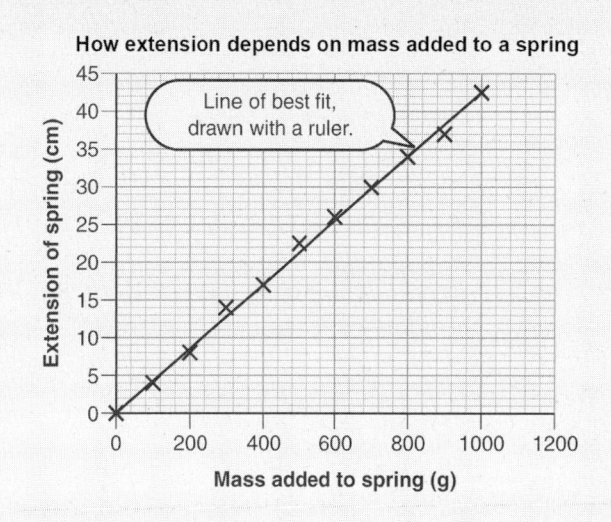

How extension depends on mass added to a spring
(Line of best fit, drawn with a ruler.)

More lines of best fit

Sometimes a graph needs two lines of best fit, and sometimes a line of best fit is curved.

How the temperature of water depends on heating time
- Here is a line of best fit for the first part of the graph.
- Join the two lines with a smooth curve.
- This is a line of best fit for the last few points.

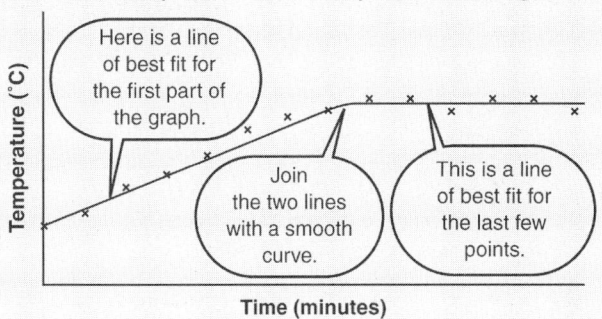

How treacle viscosity depends on temperature
- This is NOT the best line to draw on this graph.
- Draw a smooth curve through the points.

If you need to draw a curve, hold the paper so that your arm is on the inside of the curve. Use your elbow as a pivot and practise drawing the curve a few times before putting your pencil onto the paper.

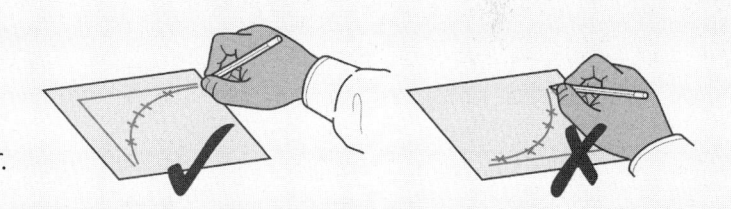

S19 Mathematical equations (Core Skills 17 (and 1))

A mathematical **equation** is a rule that connects different quantities. (If it does not contain numbers it is often called a formula.)

For example, this is the equation for calculating **speed**.

$$\text{speed} = \frac{\text{distance}}{\text{time}} \quad \text{or} \quad S = \frac{D}{T}$$

Top Tip
The quantity on its own is the subject.

Sometimes you know the speed and the time, and you want to calculate the distance the object has travelled. You rearrange the equation to make 'distance' the subject. Here are two ways of doing this. Choose whichever is easier for you.

Skills appendix

KS3 Science Lab Book

Method 1

We want D as the subject. So we want to get rid of T. At the moment, we have 'divide by T'.	$S = \dfrac{D}{T}$
To remove 'divide by T', we use its inverse, which is 'multiply by T'. We need to perform this operation on both sides of the equals sign.	$S \times T = \dfrac{D}{T} \times T$
'Divide by T' and 'multiply by T' are inverses, so they cancel each other out.	$S \times T = \dfrac{D}{\cancel{T}} \times \cancel{T}$

We are left with:

$S \times T = D$ which is the same as $D = S \times T$

The other way (**Method 2**) is to use the speed equation in the form of a triangle.

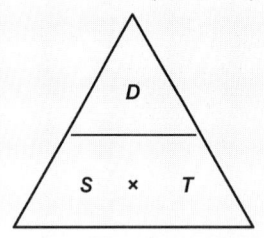

If you want to calculate the speed, you cover up the **S**:

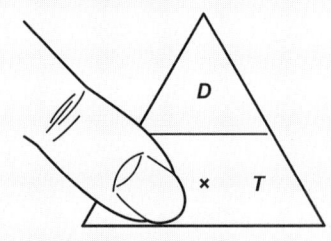

You can see $\dfrac{D}{T}$. So, the equation you need is:

$S = \dfrac{D}{T}$ (or speed = $\dfrac{\text{distance}}{\text{time}}$)

If you want to calculate the distance, you cover up the **D**:

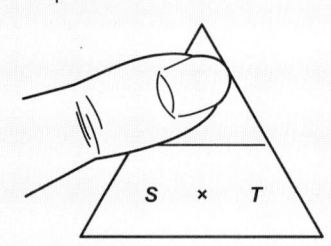

Now you can see **S × T**. So, the equation you need is:

D = S × T (or distance = speed × time)

S20 Calculating perimeters, areas and volumes (Core Skill 17)

Perimeters

The **perimeter** of a shape is the length around its outside.

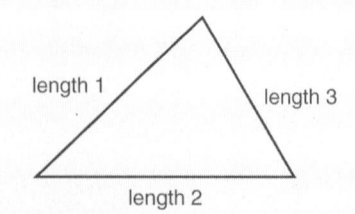

perimeter = length 1 + length 2 + length 3

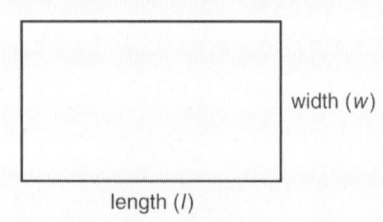

perimeter = 2*l* + 2*w*

Areas

The mathematical **equations** below the shapes show how to calculate their areas. Remember that area is measured in square units, such as m² or cm².

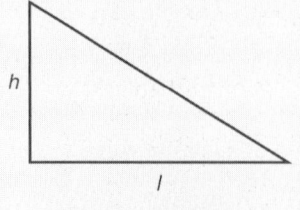

This only works for a right-angled triangle. Split other triangles up into right angled triangles to calculate their area.

area = ½ *l* × *h*

area = *l* × *h*

Glossary: www.pearsonschools.co.uk/KS3LabGlossary

Skills appendix   KS3 Science Lab Book

To calculate the area of an irregular shape, such as a leaf, draw round the shape on squared paper. Then count the squares inside your outline. Count squares that are more than half way across the outline (into your shape). Do not count squares that are less than half way into your shape. This gives an **estimate** of the area. The smaller the graph squares, the more accurate the estimate.

Volumes

The equation below the cuboid shows how to calculate its volume. Remember that volume is measured in cubic units, such as m^3 or dm^3.

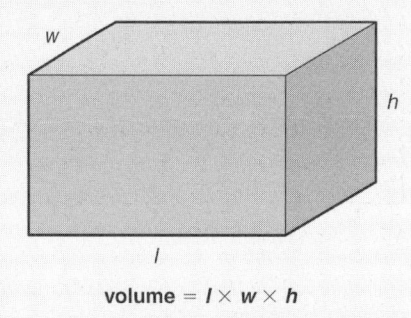

$$\text{volume} = l \times w \times h$$

S21 Averages (Core Skills 18 (and 11, 21))

The type of average that is most commonly used in science is the **mean**.

To calculate the mean:

Step 1: Add up all the **data** values. *Step 2*: Divide by the number of values.

For example, the mean of 3, 5, 7, 4, 11 is:

$$\frac{(3+5+7+4+11)}{5} = \frac{30}{5} = 6$$

> The other types of average are:
> **median** – the middle value when the values are put in numerical order
> **mode** – the most common value.

We often calculate the mean of repeated measurements. This helps to average out errors caused by errors in the measurements. The mean of the results is usually more **accurate** than one of the results.

However, if you have any **anomalous** values (values that do not fit a pattern) you often ignore them when calculating the mean. (See section S24.)

S22 Decimal places and significant figures (Core Skills 19 (and 11))

Readings are never exact, and some measuring devices are less exact than others. For example, most bathroom scales measure to the nearest 100 g, but kitchen scales measure to 1 g. The kitchen scales are more accurate, but we do not always need this degree of accuracy.

In an experiment, you need to choose measuring devices that are accurate enough for you to draw a conclusion.

Decimal places show a value's accuracy. This is the number of digits after the decimal point. For example:

| Mass of a student = 45.4 kg | 1 decimal place |
| Mass of a student = 45.432 kg | 3 decimal places |

Significant figures also show a value's accuracy. For example:

| Mass of a student = 45.4 kg | 3 significant figures |
| Mass of a student = 45.432 kg | 5 significant figures |

The second value is more accurate, but we do not need this degree of accuracy for a person's mass.

Glossary: www.pearsonschools.co.uk/KS3LabGlossary

This table shows how to change two example numbers to 2 significant figures.

A Starting from the left, find the first digit that is not a zero. Then count the number of significant figures you want (e.g. two).	165 789 The two significant figures are 16.	0.0025194 The two significant figures are 25.
B Look at the next digit and round it up if you need to.	165 789 The next digit is 5, so increase the digit before it by 1.	0.0025194 Next digit is 1, so we make no changes.
C Convert all the numbers after your last significant figure to 0s.	170 000	0.0025 If the last significant figure is a **decimal**, you do not need to write down any numbers after this figure.

In calculations, we should give answers to the same number of significant figures as the values we use.

For example:

Calculate the **speed** of a car that travels 96 km in 2.5 hours.

$$\text{speed} = \frac{\text{distance}}{\text{time}} = \frac{96}{2.5} = 38.4 \text{ km/h}$$

speed = 38 km/h   (to 2 s.f.)

S23 Correlations and relationships (Core Skills 20 (and 16))

A **correlation** or **relationship** is a link between two **variables**. As one variable changes, so does the other. You look for correlations using a **scatter graph**. If the points form a straight line, there is a type of correlation called a **linear relationship**.

A linear relationship can be:

- positive (as one variable increases, so does the other)
- negative (as one variable increases, the other decreases).

A special type of linear relationship forms a straight line that goes through the origin. This is a **directly proportional relationship**. In this relationship, if one variable doubles so does the other. We say that one variable is directly proportional to the other.

Glossary: www.pearsonschools.co.uk/KS3LabGlossary

Skills appendix

KS3 Science Lab Book

The closer the points are to a **line of best fit**, the stronger the correlation. If there are many points a long way from the line of best fit, the correlation is weak.

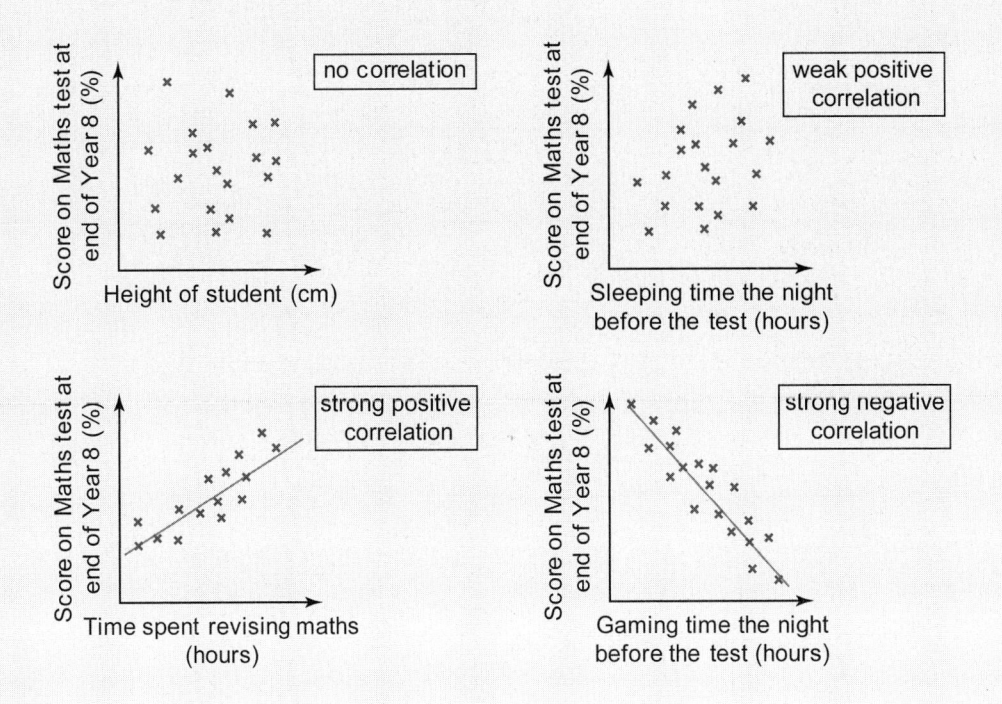

Gradients

Sometimes it is useful to calculate the gradient (slope steepness) of the line on a graph. Here is an example.

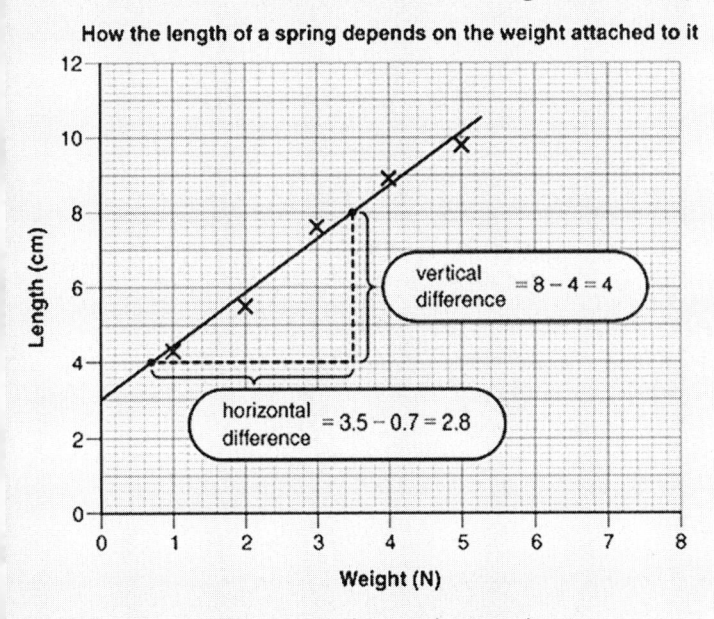

Follow these steps to work out the gradient:

A Choose *two* points on the line, where it is easy to read off the values.

B Work out the vertical difference and horizontal difference between the points.

C Divide the vertical difference by the horizontal difference:

$$\frac{4}{2.8} = 1.43$$

gradient = 1.43

Glossary: www.pearsonschools.co.uk/KS3LabGlossary

Skills appendix

S24 Errors and anomalous readings (Core Skills 21, 25)

Different kinds of error can occur when taking measurements.

Systematic errors are where all your values are shifted away from their true values by the same amount, for example if you:
- measure from the end of a ruler rather than from zero
- do not set a balance to zero before measuring a **range** of masses.

Random errors occur where chance affects some measurements and not others. This often happens because not enough care is taken over measuring, for example not allowing a thermometer time to adjust to a new temperature before recording a temperature.

Random errors can be easier to spot than systematic errors, particularly when the **data** is plotted on a graph. Random errors often stick out as **outliers** or **anomalous** readings (measurements that do not fit an overall pattern).

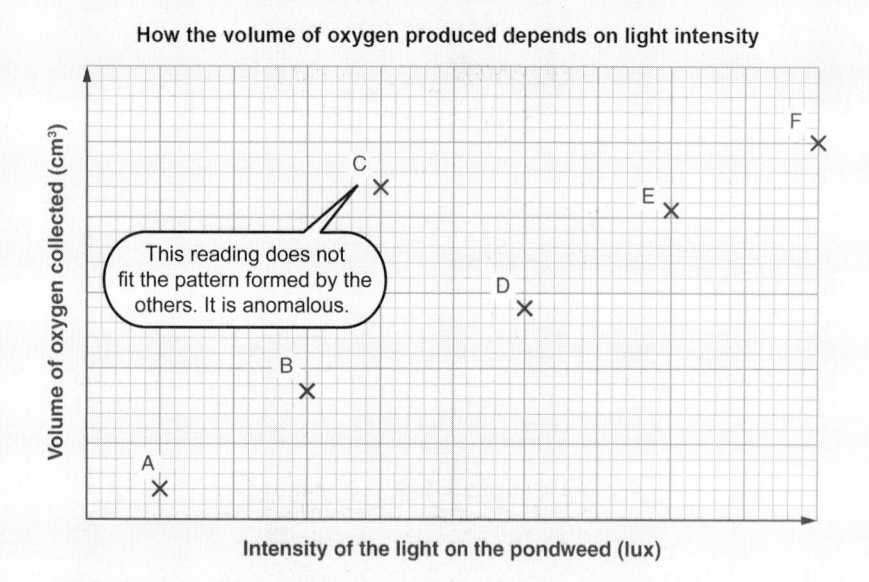

How the volume of oxygen produced depends on light intensity

Graph with Volume of oxygen collected (cm³) on y-axis and Intensity of the light on the pondweed (lux) on x-axis. Points labelled A, B, C, D, E, F. Point C is labelled: "This reading does not fit the pattern formed by the others. It is anomalous."

S25 Evaluation (Core Skills 24, 25)

When you evaluate something, you judge how good or poor it is. You also give your reasoning.

Evaluating investigations

In the evaluation section of a practical report, you judge how sure you are of your **data** and conclusion.

First, you could describe one or more of these:
- problems you had or anything that went wrong
- any **variables** that you could not control
- how **accurate** your measurements were
- how repeatable your results were (did repeated measurements give the same results?)
- how reproducible your results were (did other groups have the same results?).

Next, you use these ideas to explain how you could improve your investigation. Remember to say why your suggestions make it better.

Glossary: www.pearsonschools.co.uk/KS3LabGlossary